RECOVERY FROM HELL

Recovery from Hell

S T E V E ' H E I N Z ' N I X O N

Serendipity

First published in 2003 by
Serendipity
Suite 530
37 Store Street
Bloomsbury
London

British Library Cataloguing-in-Publication data
A catalogue record for this book is available from the British Library

ISBN 1-84394-078-7

Printed and bound in Europe by the Alden Group, Oxford

Contents

Chapter 1	Nightmare	1
Chapter 2	The Blindhouse	16
Chapter 3	Veteran's Stories	30
Chapter 4	Memories and Travels	40
Chapter 5	The Bike Ride	58
Chapter 6	Arctic Training and More Biking	76
Chapter 7	It's All Greek to Me	89
Chapter 8	Personal Accounts	97
Chapter 9	American Life	114
Chapter 10	The Final Chapter	122

Illustrations

1 Steve on his elbow crutches in 1993

2 A young Steve at the end of the Tarzan course on the 30ft wall

3 Ray and his tamdem master

4 Steve down south with his proud Mam and Dad after receiving his Gulf war medal

5 Steve with Jimmy, who performed the emergency tracheotomy

6 Steve and the lads in Texas

7 Tony and Steve at the Gym

8 Steve at Otterburn with Cpl Rennie

9 Grant and Steve on the first Bike Ride from London to Brighton

10 A cold place to stay for the night

11 Cammed out in Norway

12 Patrolling the icy roads

13 Being picked up by a chopper

14 Grant Cooper with Steve on the second Bike Ride with the new trike

Acknowledgements

Many thanks are greatly appreciated to the following:
Royal Marines Commmando Sgt Bill Wright: Currently serving
(interviewed)
Royal Marines Commmando RMR Tyne Jimmy Haley:
Retired (interviewed)
Royal Marines Commmando RMR Tyne Dave Lindsey: Retired
Royal Marines Commmando RMR Tyne Ian Robson: Retired
Royal Marines Commmando RMR Tyne Jeff Rundle:
Medically discharged
Royal Marines Commmando RMR Tyne Major Robinson:
Currently serving.

Special appreciation to all St Dunstaners:
Ray Sheriff, served in the Para's (interviewed)
Ray Hazan, served in the Royal Anglian Regiment (interviewed)
Steve Sparks, served as a Royal Marine Commando
(interviewed)
Tony Heskey, served as a Royal Marine Commando
(interviewed)
Tom Roddy, served in the Royal Air Force (interviewed),
Tony Watson, served in the Royal Navy (interviewed)
Gary 'Glasses' Lomas, served in the Royal Engineers attached
to 3 Cdo Bde (interviewed)
Billy Baxter, served in the Royal Artillery (interviewed)
Nigel Whitley, served in the Royal Navy (interviewed)
Also thanks to – Fred Bentley, Ian Millard, Steve Pendleton
and Dave Powell.

Also special thanks to Chris Chip Stilton. Chip served in the Fleet Air Arm gun crew and assists at HMS *Sultan* (interviewed). Apparently he is an expert diver!

Paddy Shelley, (interviewed) Physiotherapist, and to all medical staff in the world.

Mr Bob Ostler a former District Manager with Alico (interviewed)

Kev and Jan for the photographs

Tony for assisting with correspondence

Also thanks to Simon Rodgers of St Dunstans

Mr and Mrs Dixon for their splendid knowledge

Phil from College for his spelling techniques

Special thanks go to Mike Sullivan for proceeding to edit the fabulous and totally fantastic book.

This book was written personally by me using the computer. The interviews were carried out by me independently, using just my friends' stories. When you consider that I have limited sight difficulties, co-ordination problems, and wrote with the use of one arm and one finger, it has proved to be a remarkable achievement.

Dedicated to my late Mother and my Father. Also my gorgeous daughter Lindsey Adele; she is terrific

About the Author

Steve Nixon was born in 1969 and educated at St Roberts catholic school. On leaving school he found employment on a Youth Training Scheme at a warehouse making Christmas paper. From there he went into a carpet shop, before gaining full time employment in a supermarket chain. Whilst participating in his role he did join the Royal Marine Reserve where he earned his Green Beret after completing a rigorous one year course. Additionally he worked for an insurance company where he was actually the manager before signing up with 3 Commando Brigade on Operation Haven. Steve remains very motivated and attends a gym frequently also going out with friends and occasionally girls.

The Author wrote this book independently and carried out the interviews despite serious injuries, including being visually impaired.

Foreword

I first met Steve Nixon at St Dunstan's, Ovingdean soon after he joined the organisation, when I presented him with his St Dunstan's badge. Someone had kindly invited me to do this as I had been his Brigade Commander in North Iraq in 1991 during Operation SAFE HAVEN. I hadn't met Steve in Iraq, but I had, of course, heard about his horrific accident and his evacuation to Germany. At St Dunstan's, in addition to his lack of anything approaching normal sight he could not then stand unsupported, let alone walk, and speech was very difficult for him. He was still wresting with coming to terms with his injuries, with a new and unwelcome way of life, and more generally with the lousy and unexpected hand of cards that he had been dealt. Yet even then it was apparent that Steve was a huge person in his own right – massively proud of being a Royal Marine and fiercely determined to win, despite the cards in his hand.

Since then Steve and I have got to know each other well. I have followed his Recovery From Hell with great admiration. Of course he has had his dark moments, but he always comes booming through with a smile on his face and with a thoroughly positive attitude. Steve has faced, fought with and overcome personal challenges that most of us never experience and find difficult to even understand. He is by no means an angel, and he would certainly never pretend to be one, but he has set a powerful example over more than a decade of how to face and conquer real adversity.

This is a book of personal triumph over tragedy – a story told in his own words by a man who knows what it is to be afraid and to live in a dark and unknown world of suffering. It is also a story of relentless, raw courage, and of a fierce come-what-may determination to overcome an apparently overwhelming collection of difficulties and disappointments.

I salute Steve Nixon and his achievements – and hope that once you have read this book you will too.

Major General Andrew Keils CB CBE
Council Member, St Dunstan's

CHAPTER 1

Nightmare

We stopped to refuel on the right, which is the opposite side to the UK and consequently we were not familiar with it. My Oppo (Buddy) had run round the rear of the Land Rover to retrieve the Gerry can which held the fuel. I then slid out of the jeep and walked about two feet, and then it happened.

It hit me like a battering ram, I was literally lifted from the road with my head throbbing with pain and blood already gushing out of my head wounds. About 200 yards on, I came crashing onto the dusty road. There I lay, my head spinning, I could hardly breathe. I heard a voice screaming 'Heinz, Heinz', coming closer by the second. It was obviously my oppo, Washington. He was shouting my nickname.

He reached me, sweat running down his shaven head, from the heat rather than physical exertion. Immediately he placed me in the recovery position and encouraged me to breathe. The blood was making quite a pretty design on the road. Then a loud, very familiar engine noise was becoming steadily louder by the second. I was semi-conscious so Washington and I both heard it. Cpl Washington then sprinted, as if he was still in training, into the centre of the road (if you could call it a road) and waved his arms, informing the MOD vehicle to stop. The MOD jeep was in fact a small ambulance. Cpl Washington briefed the ambulance driver like the professional he was. With a struggle I was loaded on board. I felt drowsy and sick. Washington looked at me and then said to the other two men that we had better find a hospital and fast. He then flagged down the rest of the Packet (convoy, column) and informed them there had been an RTA.

I was slowly losing consciousness and the lads knew they had to find a hospital and fast, as after a serious brain injury the brain swells, hence speed is essential. The MOD driver introduced himself as Jimmy and was constantly talking to me and encouraging me to breathe; talking to me about why we were there. Jimmy then received the services from an English speaking Turk who was very helpful. I began to mumble, and spray and splutter blood. I couldn't breathe and I was going down big-style. Jimmy was overjoyed when I fell into a deep sleep but his shrieks of delight nearly woke me up.

We continued driving along the dusty road, and then it happened. I woke up coughing blood. My head was shaking and I had lost a tremendous amount of blood. I was coughing and spluttering blood again. This time Jimmy had to make a decision and he penetrated my neck with a sharp object. It was an emergency tracheotomy. He saved my life. Cheers mate!

We then spotted what looked like a hospital. It seemed like we were the only humans on the planet. All the packet waited outside as only a few were allowed in, but we were horrified to see cats' shit and dried blood on the operating table.

Then we stopped at another hospital but before I could be seen, payment had to be mastered. The lads quickly fumbled through their pockets but as they were in the field they carried little or no money. They managed to scrape the payment together. The Turks mustered treatment and what they actually did was to patch me up very well, until I could receive the correct treatment.

I then was loaded back into the ambulance and driven off to find a suitable head injury hospital, because up to now we hadn't found one.

All the lads thought I was dead or that I wouldn't make it. I nearly didn't. I died six times on the way to receiving treatment and Jimmy revived me every time. I sympathize with Jimmy because I was in a hell of a mess, even after the Turks had stitched me up, but they had done exceptionally well under the circumstances. We then met a switched-on Captain who took one look at me and then called in a chopper. The lads made an LZ where a chopper could land (don't forget it was late at night and the weather was turning rotten) so the lads had to be extra quick. I was casevacted into Germany. Once there I slipped into a coma as if I had been waiting to arrive, and then our maker had said 'All right Heinz you are safe, now go to sleep'.

My parents came out to see me, even though this was unusual, but what was more unusual, the MOD had allowed my girlfriend, with whom I had a daughter, to see me. My daughter's name is Lindsey Adele and she is 15 years old. The MOD obviously thought I was going to die and that's why they had paid for my dependants to fly out to see me for the very last time, but fortunately it turned out not to be!

My Father marched in, like the proud man he was, took one look at me and collapsed unconscious. He had been blacking out for some time and the medical staff of the UK did not have a clue what was actually causing it. He ended up with a German pacemaker. It's ironic really. We beat them in two World Wars and yet my Dad has to go to Germany, to find out why he is having difficulties. My Mother was overjoyed with relief and now she prayed for her son. Sadly my Mother passed away four and a half years ago. She was one of the people I received my inspiration from. My Dad tried to find out where I had received all the gashes. Apparently I had raised my arms to try and save my face. This theory made sense and my Dad was satisfied.

The doctors and nurses cleaned me up very well, so much so I was like a new man.

Again the doctors commented on what an excellent job the Turks had done. My poor Mother had two of her family down and out. My Dad was funny as he had the drip attached to his body. His bed space was covered with correspondence and it looked like JR's desk in *Dallas*. One of the doctors just looked at my Mam and shook his head as if to say, you are a brick. It was time to casevac me back to the UK I had stayed in Germany long enough. As we left the nurses told my Mum to take some photographs so when I recovered she could compare them, but she would have none of it. Well, if I would ever make any improvements, if I would ever walk again, nobody knew at that very early point in time.

My Dad continued to talk to me as he had been instructed to. What I didn't realize about being in a coma is that you can still hear, consequently that's why I can still talk and have still got my memory. Well that's my theory, and nobody has got any medical evidence to prove otherwise. Also, with a little bit help from upstairs, if you know what I mean.

A roar of the engine and we were airborne quite quickly, moving through the clouds. On board the plane I received round-the-clock treatment. I would have felt like Royalty if I'd known. I was still in a coma and bleeding from my face wounds. The pilot was about to take me down south as this was the normal routine but I would have been a long way from home. My Dad managed to persuade the pilot to change course, well obviously. Good skills, Dad. Consequently I was flown to Newcastle Airport and actually transferred to the General Hospital Special Head Injury ward. Before I go any further with the story I want to get one thing straight. A very serious head injury is in fact a fully closed brain injury and it stops you doing almost every single thing in your life. You can still have sex though, thank God!

My Uncle Brian came to meet the Hercules and the ground staff wanted to know how he knew there was a military Hercules landing. When he explained, it was okay.

I came to Newcastle because all my friends and family were in the north-east and they would all play a big part in my recovery from hell. There, I would receive my encouragement, although I didn't need much. My friend Jeff Rundle, who was in the Royal Marines with me, said to me 'Heinz, I have a hell of a lot of faith in you. You'll do it'. When I think back, I didn't know where I was, actually but I remember having dreams and I believe that because my family and friends were praying, that's why I am so well. I was christened a Catholic but I don't attend Church, although I still believe.

I was actually dreaming, in fact having nightmares, about the whole rotten business, and I was still unconscious at this point. The physiotherapists came for me each day and they placed me over a large ball and I couldn't keep my balance, but looking back I didn't have much say in the matter because I was still in a coma. This is pretty acceptable because if the physio hadn't bothered with me I would have been a cabbage. All the hard work paid off.

There were a tremendous number of visitors and I think they all liked the Royal Marines. One particular man called Keith commented it was the first time he had ever seen me quiet. My other mate, Jeff said well Heinz could talk under water, but now he wished I would. The lads were queuing up at visiting times and a schoolmate stood patiently and quite frequently had to return home unable to see me because all the Marines were in. Cheers Fos and lads! Only a few were allowed in at any one time. I had a punctured lung and a gash where my lung had been penetrated to enable the fluid to drain off. They had made a small insertion into my stomach to give me food. I came out of the coma in the General to shrieks of delight from everybody around.

My Dad said that according to the medical staff at the General I was out of the coma after nearly 4 months, but my Dad informs me I was like a rag doll. Actually it seemed much longer because I didn't know where I was or what had really occurred. I can only recall my friend taking me for a walk in the grounds and nearly putting me back in a coma, as I fell out of the bloody wheelchair. Little did I know, in years to come I would learn to detest the 'Four-Wheeled Monster'. Let's be serious, it looks hideous and resembles a kid's pushchair. After that escapade a band was attached round my head and fitted around the 'Monster' to stop me doing somersaults. The nurses were very impressed with my fitness and, even more, how I'd managed to survive after such a life threatening experience. The nurses told my Mam that if I hadn't been so exceptionally fit I surely would have perished.

When I left school I joined a small gym which went by the name of Woodstone Body Builders. The owner, Brian, used to organize Body Building Competitions and Shows etc

I was always fit and a keen sportsman. It was Brian

who gave me the name Heinz, and this continued with Jeff and the Marines using it. My Dad was very fit in his younger days and we all did the Great North Run. My Dad completed the first ever Great North Run in 1981 and was the instigator in me running it the very next year. My sister and her friend also completed the race. I used to train hard, and that's why I'm alive and have done so well.

Back at the General Hospital, one of the nurses asked me if I wanted to go outside. I remembered the last time I went out with a friend. Outside had nearly killed me. At that time any slight movement used to drain me and I needed plenty of liquids. I spent over four months at the General and I still don't remember much as most of the time I was sleeping (14 weeks in a coma). My parents told me about the General but most of it is a blur as at this point I could have been on the bloody moon for all I knew. Then I was loaded into a waiting ambulance and driven the fairly short journey past the Television Studios and into a desolate place called Hunter's Moor, which actually resembled an old stately home.

In Hunter's Moor I was confused, in the very early stages I wanted to sleep all the time but I do remember most occurrences which took place. I actually thought I was in a Concentration Camp, but if I'd really thought about it, which Concentration Camp would treat you so well? But then I could not think. When I first arrived a man called Chris the Porter came to my bed space and informed me that he had come to collect me for physio. I did believe I was going to be interrogated. We went down a lift and along a large corridor to the Torture Chamber. At first I used to hate physiotherapy because it was painful. After lying unconscious for such a long period, my muscles had all wasted away and my left arm was all mangled and twisted.

Funnily enough most of my flesh wounds had healed, while I was in the coma. The theory was that while I was sleeping, they had had the chance to heal, and this made me feel better. There were only a few scars but these were barely visible. At the beginning I used to have four meals a day in the sun lounge, because I had food all over Newcastle. It was pathetic the way I couldn't even hold my knife and fork correctly, all through a damn truck. I soon realized that I couldn't do the simplest tasks in everyday life. For example I could not even sit up without using my arms. It seems quite simple to actually sit up and balance but I was a wreck and had been nearly killed.

My Uncle Brian came in one day with a group of visitors and I mumbled a hello to every one except Ned. This was my Uncle's nickname. He was called Ned because his surname is Kelly, hence the criminal Ned Kelly who was transported to Australia.

'What about me Steve!' he said, I said 'I didn't even see you.' From that day on I knew I was half-blind, but that this would improve dramatically. Another morning at Hunter's Moor and the porter came wobbling along the ward, obviously still pissed from the alcohol abuse of the night before. 'Come on, let's be having you.' I was still in a quite remarkable dream about my pop idol, and she was a nurse just about to get her kit off. Anyway I was pretty pissed off. It was so degrading because I had to wait for the nurses to get me washed and dressed.

That made me reflect on my previous life just walking down the street. I had always been so professional and clean in my two jobs both as a area sales manager and a L/ CPL in the Royal Marines Reserve. I could visualize myself just walking briskly, down the street, hoping and praying that around the next corner lay my prize and if not, somewhere I could receive some warmth. How would the sales team be coping without the 'Great Heinz'? But now I kept asking myself: Where was I? What was I doing? Where ever I was, for God's sake somebody please tell me what's going on! The medical staff did and my family did and it just passed by my damaged memory. I had come to my senses but I still didn't know where I was. The nurses got me washed and dressed, with a struggle, I might add. Then Chris came in, still finishing his coffee, I heard him grumble to the nurses about something, and then we were off.

I was so confused and I kept on asking him, where are we going? He mumbled back in a broad Geordie voice, 'I'm just taking you down to physiotherapy – physio', he chanted back. Bullshit, I muttered to myself, he's taking me to that Torture Chamber again. Then this tall blonde headed man came in and he attempted to sit me on the floor, which meant I had to exit the wheelchair, which I was not prepared to do. I kept shouting about the Geneva Convention and that I had rights.

Every night I would begin to dream and at this stage I still didn't have a clue where I was or what I was doing. Morning came and this Chris took me to another room with OT on the door, and I did think it stood for Over seas Termination. Really it stood for occupational therapy, words with which I would become familiar over the coming years. Once there I started to learn exercises for my left arm, which was magnificent to what it had been.

One day at the physio department, the same blonde man stood like a gunslinger from the old Westerns, hands over the tops of his thighs as if he was ready to draw and he was waiting for me. I didn't find out until much later that the man was in fact a woman; I put this down to my eyesight! The very next day an officer from the Royal Navy came to visit me (the Royal Marines are part of the Navy).

He informed me of what had happened and I started to believe him, but I was still confused. Then all of a sudden it all came flooding back, how I'd left my job as Area Sales Manager. Well I could talk under water, according to Jeff. I was self-employed for the company American Life (ALICO) so I could take time off. We were taught PMA which stands for Positive Mental Attitude and all salesmen were instructed to be positive and professional. Above all they were taught to adapt to any situation, just like the Royal Marines.

The Sales Team were doing well and actually visiting clients who already had a policy and upgrading them to a more substantial cover.

Then at 3 days notice, I volunteered for Service with the regular Corps, 3 Commando Brigade on Operation Safe Haven. This humanitarian Operation was in aid of the Kurds of Northern Iraq. The whole packet (Convoy, Column) was lost. Consequently my Land Rover had sprung an oil leak, so that's why I had to double up with CPL Washington in his Jeep.

So far so good, and then a short, stroppy man came sprinting up and he informed us they must have taken a wrong turning or else someone had fucked up the signs. We were then tasked to find the correct route. Washington drove as I read the map; we had stopped to refuel, and then a loud thud. The 4-ton truck racing away, at no point did it break its momentum. As you can imagine I was a mangled wreck.

The Royal Navy Officer continued to speak as I reflected the story in my mind. I just could not comprehend why and how it possibly happened. I was the last person anyone would have dreamed would get injured. I was the loudest, bubbliest person in ALICO, and that transferred over to the Royal Marines reserve. The most ironic thing is, what I had preached, consequently happened to me.

The officer left, leaving a desolate silence hanging over the sun lounge. I was furious with myself for allowing myself to sign up in the first damned place, but then I remembered I had only been 21. It was an adventure and I had wanted to help the starving Kurds. I would have gone anyway, so I just put it down to circumstances and doing the job.

That same afternoon I was sitting on my bed and Chris the porter appeared as if he'd just landed with a gust of wind. This time we were going back to OT (occupational therapy).

I arrived to find the OT teacher doing some sort of embroidery. She pointed to a door and as it was late afternoon she was obviously going home. Then I enquired 'What about me?' She replied 'Simjim is with you, Stephen.' Simjim was a foreigner. He took me into a side room and he said, 'Can you dress yourself yet?' I thought he was taking the piss. I had shouted back, 'I've had a bloody accident, I'm not 2', but I was in the Medical staff's eyes because I had to learn every single thing again. It was so degrading and pathetic, I was dribbling like a little baby and I couldn't even dress myself at the beginning. That night a feeling came over me, I can't begin to describe properly; one of pity and hope and a sense of pride, but from that minute on I kept improving. I said to myself that I'd do it, even if it killed me. I was so dedicated and determined it was untrue. From that day forward it was my job. Recovery! Recovery!

That afternoon Chris appeared in the sun lounge. I don't know why it was called the bloody sun lounge, as there was never any sun. I had noticed he was there for other patients. Next morning I was woken up by the nurses and there he was again. I felt like he had been beamed down from the flippin' moon.

That very next morning as quick as you like, I was washed and dressed and then helped into the 'Monster' and driven down to physiotherapy. I quickly got to grips with the exercises shown to me. First of all I had to apologize to the woman whom I had mistaken for a man. I stated that I had been horribly confused and that I had not known where I was, but she just said 'It's okay Stephen, you've had a serious brain injury and that is a common factor after a serious head injury.' Especially one like I had received.

From that day forward we got on very well and it was her I've got to thank for actually putting me in touch with my current success story. Progressing on and that afternoon Chris was there again, I began to think he fancied me! He collected me from the sun lounge and we proceeded up the elevator, crossed over the corridor and into a square room. I thought I was on bloody playschool. A woman stood in the doorway, thanked Chris and continued to manoeuvre me and the Chariot into a free space in the room.

Once settled in the square room she began by asking my name and where I had lived and she actually said I spoke very good English. She continued to test my speech and that was my first introduction to speech therapy. Now it was time for bed. That part of rehabilitation I did enjoy, sleeping, because after a brain/head injury, you use 3 times as much energy as everyone else. Consequently when I trained at the Gym I was in fact using three times as much energy as everyone else, so in a fact I was beating them, but it was ever so hard, I was hanging out.

I met a physio assistant who knew his stuff, a *Sunderland* supporter called Martin. There was a patient whose husband had free tickets for the Sunderland versus Millwall game in the Executive Boxes that coming Saturday. Me, Martin and Jenny who was my physiotherapist went along. I was ecstatic as we met all the players, but what was really superb was that we won, a smashing 4–2.

The OT continued and the speech therapy, but with little emphasis on my eyesight. The most essential part of my rehabilitation was my mobility. Well at that time, like quite a number of the general public, I had not heard of St Dunstans. St Dunstans were to admit me and consequently build me a bungalow. They have been exceptional. At the physio department they were so impressed with me they used to give me extra physio. All my movements were jammed up but I did manage to walk with the aid of a Zimmer frame, though I was still using the wheelchair a tremendous amount of the time.

Then I progressed down to the dining room so it meant I could feed myself. Physio continued and soon afterwards I returned over the river to live with my parents.

My Dad believed in me. I started my recovery when I walked out of Ned's car and into the house, with the aid of a Zimmer frame, and I felt as low as my feet. I felt conspicuous walking in, knowing everybody would be watching me, purely out of interest, I might add.

My mother was so overjoyed with emotion that her No 1 son was back home. That's not taking anything away from my younger brother. It's just I was hatched first.

Next day and I still needed a small bit of support with

general tasks. I used to stand six inches away from the door and when I lost my balance my Dad would push me back against the door so that I could correct my balance and actually walk. Before going outside I had to master walking in the house and I used to walk three times round the track. Well what that actually means is when we were children me, my cousin and my brother used to play 'three times round the track'. You all chose a car and then you would throw the dice and move your car using the ruler, moving your car how many spaces you scored. First to get round three times was the winner. It was a brilliant game and I didn't think for one minute that I would be walking round as part of my recovery from hell. My Dad and me did a tremendous amount of physio and exercise in the house.

When we first went outside the going was tough. The pavements were not straight and trying to go downhill was terrible, but my Dad had a solution, in fact my Dad had a solution for almost every single thing. It was not bad going up hills but trying to walk downhill was so difficult. You don't think about it, but when you're injured it takes some deliberate concentration. Watching TV was difficult when you're half-blind. Well I managed. I used to buy videos that I had already seen previous to the injury, so consequently I could follow the story.

I can't begin to describe my eyesight; it does look to the naked eye as if there is absolutely nothing wrong. Although I was away from the hospital I was still attending physio. Royal Marines, who I'd gone through training with, were working at the Unit so they used to pick me up. It was like my own private ambulance. One day when I was attending physio my Dad received a phone call from a Major Manx who stated that he was from St Dunstans and they had a place available for me.

My Dad said 'What if Steve doesn't want to go?' and the reply was 'This is a posting!' When I came in I was furious with my Dad because I was still serving and the MOD could have sent me to Timbuktu if they wanted to, but no pressure was put on me in the slightest, so I decided to go of my own free will.

CHAPTER 2

The Blind House

St Dunstans used a firm that operated a fleet of vehicles to ferry men up and down the country. St D's had their own squad of cars but unfortunately they didn't come that far North 12 years ago. The driver could not drive a car. How the hell he ever passed his test, I do not know. He was jerking the clutch every gear change and braking like he was stopping a tank. It must have been his age. He introduced himself as Mark and we got on fairly well but he drove like there was a copper up his arse.

We stopped at a depot in Birmingham to refuel and I asked Mark to tell me about St Dunstans, because like the majority of the population I hadn't heard of it.

Sir Arthur Pearson formed St Dunstans in 1915 during World War I. It was originally established for the men returning from the war, suffering from blindness caused by mustard gas or any other eye injuries. He told me about Fred Bentley who is a St Dunstaner and it was his son Colin who had the contract for ferrying the men up and down the country. Colin had a depot in Birmingham.

Fred was a member of the DLI (Durham Light Infantry). Fred told me he was injured attacking the German positions during World War II. He is an incredible man and he informed me of the DLI'S nickname which is the Dirty Little Imps.

It was a long and very tiresome journey and it took over eight hours including the stop at Birmingham. The

16

thing is that, because my eyes were damaged, I could not travel long journeys. They made me feel sick and dizzy, so the solution was to travel by air but I was fine for short distances.

When we arrived it was late at night so most of the staff had already left for the evening. But there were still ample staff to cater for my needs, which miraculously were not many, once I was in my room. It was superb because you had an en suite, drinking facilities and an alarm system that relayed you back to an orderly. Next morning I was assisted by the Wing 1 Orderly, Peter Wiltshire, who was in fact the headman, although he didn't receive the wages or recognition that he was due. He had worked as an orderly since he was nineteen and was very experienced at his job.

I was introduced to a Colonel Bray, who was firm but fair. The place was gigantic and was designed in the shape of an aircraft. There was a swimming pool, which was very beneficial for my recovery from Hell. I obviously took the plunge about twice a week but they also had a gym, which I preferred because I liked training, it was in the blood. They have archery, and although it is hard to believe that totally blind men can fire arrows, they can, but are always supervised. There are some pretty damned good shots and some have won great competitions. They have a training department and that consisted of a cookery department, a workshop, handicraft room and a typing room, when I was in training. Of course it's all changed now and there's a lot more emphasis on nursing care. Now they have a computer department. One person who has been there a while is the Sports and Recreation Manager, Grant Cooper. His job is keeping every one fit and active, and organizing fund-raising events. He also runs the pool and indoor and outdoor activities. Currently a fantastic lady called Louise runs the Sports department. When I was in training, a man called Mr Myagie ran the swimming pool and it was his pride and joy. You were instructed to walk on the right because of all the veterans who had been blinded.

After my little tour I was shown the dining room. I didn't have much time after breakfast. The first thing I noticed is the way in which the staff were so friendly. I settled in quite well and soon after I arrived, another young lad arrived called Steve Pendleton who had been injured in Northern Ireland. He was a member of the Royal Green Jackets. He had a wooden leg and was half-blind. I got knocked down and nearly killed and he was engaged in a chopper crash and nearly killed – we are a right pair! Lessons continued to a high degree. When I first started training there was little or no equipment in the gym. You had the locals who lived near to St Dunstans who had stayed and settled there after the Second World War.

Grant and I worked well together. I joined an injury group and on a Wednesday a very tired Grant and I used to go up to Lewis Prison to weight train. The Cons used to assist and sometimes we would go for a quick beer afterwards. Col Bray organized a private physiotherapist, and I quickly got to grips with the exercises demonstrated. Sometimes we attempted physio in the pool, which was a real laugh and of course Grant assisted. Peter Wiltshire, the Wing One orderly, actually took away my wheelchair and I was happy about this because it would enable me to walk with my Zimmer frame. Peter was very efficient at his job and so caring for the St Dunstaners. One thing that became apparent to everyone was the fact I had very poor balance, and the old men who were totally blind used to walk fast so consequently we would meet on a collision course and I would be on the losing side and fall to the ground. Also I used to fall on everyone's food. One particular day I lost my temper and a guy called George ended up with custard all over him. There were a lot more men in the olden days and it was exceptionally busy.

St Dunstans has an HQ in London. One person who works at the HQ is Ray Hazan and he works as the overall Manager for public relations. Actually Ray is a former member of the Royal Anglian Regiment.

Ray spoke about his Army career and how he was injured, resulting in total blindness and the loss of his right hand and also a high amount of hearing difficulties. He is a very courageous man and does a tremendous amount of assistance towards all St Dunstaners. Ray spoke to me with reference to his Army Career:

The thought of working in a office did not appeal to me. At School I passed all the Civil Servants Exams and this enabled me to work for the War Office Selection Board. Consequently a place at Sandhurst was available. This is the Officer Training College and I could see myself being a soldier. Our two year course culminated with a visit to our Commissioning Parade by our Majesty the Queen in June 1965.

I became a Second Lieutenant in the 2nd Battalion the Royal Anglian Regiment.

My first posting was to Cyprus where I assumed the position of Platoon Commander, responsible for the training and welfare of up to 30 soldiers. Boring guard duties progressed at an ammunition dump, sadly it was in the middle of nowhere. The RAF were extremely busy with desert training in Libya.

I returned to the UK after enjoying a RAF

indulgence flight to the West Coast of America for the quite low and amusing figure of £2 and 18 shillings. I was then sent to Northampton for 18 months. I assisted the Army Youth Team which consisted of an Officer in charge, a Sgt and a further 3 soldiers a small independent Command. We were tasked to organize activities for the candidates, 'this consisted of trampoline, rock climbing, gym pursuits) within Northamptonshire, not in a direct recruiting role, but to encourage youngsters who would consider an Army career. It was a fascinating and rewarding period. The challenge of getting a 16 year old, self-conscious male and to instruct them was more challenging than commanding soldiers. Then I rejoined the 2nd Battalion of the Royal Anglian Regiment to become Intelligence Officer. I was responsible for plotting enemy and friendly missions in action etc. It was a role I was not best suited to but I still managed to enjoy exercises in Malaya and Kenya during this period. The Battalion was acting portable role; we were part of 3 Division based in Colchester so we had to be ready to deploy and hence the variety of training and preparation.

I was married in September 1965 to a beautiful and caring woman, who is absolutely wonderful. Six weeks later I was off to Northern Ireland for the first time. It wasn't a very pleasant start when my Company Commander committed suicide before the remainder of the Company arrived. I was second in command and I manned the ops room for 12–14 hours a day, been in contact constantly with the OC, Patrols and the Battalion HQ. It was a difficult time over there, especially with a new wife, and sadly contact had to be written correspondence only.

Between my two Tours of Northern Ireland I had two very stable years at the Junior Infantry Battalion. My intended job of Training Officer was civilianized just before I arrived so I was given the position of Second in Command, OC Driver and Training and Sports Officer. We purchased our first home in Folkestone where we enjoyed 6 months of civilian life before I was off on my second tour of Northern Ireland, This time in Blighs Lane on the edge of the notorious Creggan estate in Londonderry.

We were billeted in a warehouse that made wiring for cars. In 1973 a General visited, and he was objecting to having British soldiers in their grounds. A parcel which had been delivered a few days earlier had been mis-delivered to the factory. It had been intercepted and then it was fitted with a time device and was given to one of the General's bodyguards.

At that time the Ops room was being manned by a 2nd Lt. He was attached to us to gain some valuable infantry experience. The Company Commander was away supporting the Company Football team, so I thought I had better be present in case he called in unexpectedly.

I asked the soldier where he had got the parcel from? It was 12 inches long, 6 inches wide and 3 inches deep. It was from Letraset and was addressed to the Chief Clerk of a nearby Gunner Regiment. As I was holding it to my left hand and speaking to the soldier, suddenly it exploded and all went totally silent and dark. I felt, heard and could see nothing!

When I came to, I sensed something disastrous and dramatic had happened, probably connected to the parcel, and I cursed myself for having been caught out.

It was apparent that I was totally blind and my arm was a twisted wreck, not to mention my disastrous hearing difficulties. It was incredibly difficult to accept what had actually occurred. The gas cylinder fire was threatening to explode at any given time. The soldiers made the Ops room safe, whilst I was being escorted to a waiting ambulance. Second Lieutenant Dobbie was killed in the blast.

I spend a week in intensive care in hospital and my father and wife were flown out to be at my side. After some four weeks I was transferred back to the South of England and I ended up at St Dunstans at Ovingdean in Brighton!

Returning back to my own 'Recovery fro m Hell', Peter Wiltshire was asked to look after me, to which he agreed. When he was on his days off a volunteer called Lance Freeborn, a former policeman in the Royal Ulster Constabulary took over. How unusual, he was a big guy! You know that most policemen are quite tall lads; I presume they think they are going to frighten the criminals into surrendering.

Lance and I used to go swimming because after the injury I lost the ability to swim. Although I was like an athlete underwater and on my back. The swimming was superb and I could walk in the water, which assisted my balance and consequently my mobility.

Peter wasn't a strong swimmer unlike Lance but Peter was a really excellent orderly (Escort). Peter hadn't been in the Forces, so Lance got the job of escorting me on the Parade at the Cenotaph Remembrance. Peter and I used to walk around the seat at the entrance Hall just as part of my physiotherapy. We did a tremendous amount of work, even walking up the stairs took a lot of effort, and we used to do the whole five floors. Not all the time of course, but it was great for my recovery.

One particular day I was walking along the corridor using the rail. Well I could see but my eyes were definitely affected. Even now when I say 'who's that?' my mates think I'm taking the piss. I can't describe my eyesight, no optician can describe my eyes and certainly no doctor. I find it difficult to recognize features. I use the rail as a means of support and it assists with my mobility and my balance.

It was rapidly approaching Christmas 1992 and one and a half years since I had sustained a very serious brain injury. Anyway me, Peter, Steve and Steve's escort a delightful lady, yomped round Church Hill Square all day Saturday. We all purchased quite a number of very good presents. St Dunstans ran a scheduled bus service to pick up the men and workers so it was easy to return to the House.

As time progressed I found myself improving to a high degree but sadly that only continued for three years and then my improvement became painfully slow. The physio was really pleased with my progress and my mobility increased from a Zimmer frame onto two crutches and that was cool, so people would think that I'd just broken my legs, instead of being smacked by a 4-ton truck.

Well I used to return home every six or seven weeks to see family and friends. It was on one particular visit home and one night that my mate Jeff Rundle came to my parents' house to see me. I was living there until St Dunstans built me a bungalow. We had a few beers and reflected on why each of us had joined the Royal Marines in the first place. We both stated it was for the adventure and the challenge of winning a Green Beret. It was pretty tough at first and at no point did it ever get any easier.

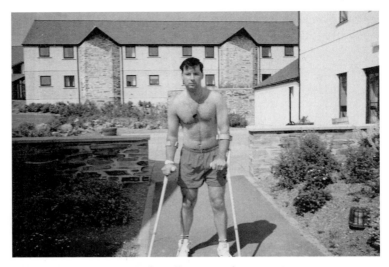

Steve on his elbow crutches in 1993

First of all we had to pass a USMC (United States Marine Corps) assessment that was a series of tests to enable the instructors to see for themselves if we were capable of achieving a Green Beret. Jeff and I both passed and what we did not know was our Troop was to receive the most passes for a long period at RMR Tyne (Royal Marine Reserve Tyne).

We both got mega fit and we used to train every spare minute we had. Going to the gym after work and running was a regular occurrence. It was entirely up to the individual, how badly he wanted a Green Beret. Unlike the Regular Corps, it was harder to get a Green Beret in the Reserve because when you came in from work you were forced to start all over again, but that's only my opinion.

Some of the instructors are pleading with you to give in but it is only to see what extreme limits you will go to that will enable you to pass the Commando Course.

A young Steve at the end of the Tarzan course
on the 30ft wall

When I achieved my Green Beret it was very tough. Actually we pass the exact same Commando Course as the Regular Commandos. The training standards have not been made flimsy in any degree, it's just you definitely have more chances to pass now. After the Falklands War in 1982 it was extremely difficult to achieve a Green Beret. I was very experienced after winning my Green Beret and after training in the United States, frequently going to Arctic Norway and then signing up with the Corps, I was pretty professional and certainly extremely fit.

Much training had passed over six months, and we were ready to attend a phase I course at the Commando Training Centre, Royal Marines. When we got home there was a sense of urgency required. We knew what to expect the very next time we attended. Jeff and I used to run along the cliffs down onto the beach and up the steps with full kit and boots. This took place on the cliffs of South Shields and another six months and then we would return again. Then down to Lympstone to be put through our paces, this time on our Commando Course for the coveted Green Beret. Both Jeff and I passed. I was told I had achieved a good pass, which I was really pleased with, but then the work really started. Sadly we are now both medically discharged through no fault of our own.

After that visit when I met Jeff again I returned down South to St Dunstans. It was a weekend and there wasn't much to do on a weekend, At least that was so 12 years ago, but I always found something to do. Two of the lads who worked there at the time actually taught me how to play chess, Well I was only 23 my education hadn't stretched that far. Steve Pendleton was leaving and going to College. Shortly after he left I left, but I was not so lucky as Steve, I found myself going to another hospital. This time to a so-called Specialist Hospital for Brain Injuries, at Ticehurst.

The St Dunstans driver pulled up in the middle of the country outside this house. It was very similar to the previous hospital I was at, Hunter's Moor. I remember this Army cook, he had apparently been admitted some time before me. I was only interested in physio because I myself and a lot of experts stated that it was the most beneficial in aid of my recovery. There was the same as the last hospital, a physiotherapist, occupational therapist and a speech therapist. Well there was obviously more but I didn't require any further treatment. It was a nice place, there was friendly staff and we were taken out to the cinema etc every so often. It was the same as the previous establishment, zero to do on a weekend. So as a result I found myself travelling the short distance back to St Dunstans at Brighton just for the weekends. Well at least I could see my friends.

The physiotherapist did achieve something for me. At St Dunstans I was walking with two crutches and then two sticks but I wasn't independent on the two sticks. When I left Ticehurst I was able to manage independently on my two sticks.

This guy called Dave and I transformed my room into a gym. Gary who used to work for St Dunstans had built me a frame and he had attached my punch bag to it. It was only used for assisting with my balance. I could hardly stand up, never mind box. Dave and I used to do a circuit. I found Dave to be pretty fit, as he was into cycling in a big way and he was a right stick insect. He was horribly thin. We used to go down the local pub in the village as part of our rehabilitation.

One other pleasure of mine was receiving visitors. My first ever visitor was none other than Major General Keils who was a very good friend and was the Operational Commander out in the Gulf. He had already presented my St Dunstans Badge and he had stated it was as important as a Military Medal and that it was a badge of Honour. He had been a Brigadier the first time I had met him; now, he was a Major General. At the time that was all I had to show for my involvement in the conflict. The Training Officer at St Dunstans came to Ticehurst and I really appreciated her visits, I used to look forward to them. The best visit was of course my parents. They stayed at the village pretty close to Ticehurst Hospital. We caught a cab down to Eastbourne.

It was a very warm day and the unusual temperatures for that time of year had brought the 'Talent' (Beautiful Women, Very fit) out in there droves. Not that I had much use for them, I could only see the outline but that was good enough. I was using the wheelchair quite a lot. I hardly use it now but I need it occasionally from time to time. It's the stigma of having everyone looking down upon you, and they always talk to the person with you. Well I still need it for long journeys, let's be realistic, I couldn't walk that far.

My Dad pushed me about, all over Eastbourne. It was great just to get the fresh air and let the sea breeze blow on our faces. The time passed quickly and soon it was time to return to get our taxi. Dave was busy painting as part of his treatment and making things. I did used to fancy some lady called Jane but sadly she was out of my league. Ironically I bumped into my old speech therapist from Ticehurst. Judy lived next to an old St Dunstaner and was visiting St Dunstans at Ovingdean, Brighton.

My parents returned home all the way back to the North East. It was a long journey and my Dad didn't travel too well after his dance with death. I said my farewells and then I was off back to St Dunstans. Dave the driver picked me up and we had become quite good pals. I asked him what was new? He told me there was another Royal Marine in training and Two Crabfats (nick-name for the Royal Air Force). We bumped into Col Bray at the entrance hall and he informed me it had been quiet without me. I just said how unusual. Well I wasn't a criminal, I was just mischievous.

St Dunstans had decided to build me a bungalow where I was from, in the Northeast. I was ecstatic but my mother had her doubts. After all I had never left home. I was shown to the fourth floor, the Trainees Wing next door to the teacher's room. The orderlies were busy polishing the floor like the Queen herself was going to inspect it. Lance and Peter were still working there. Lance had apparently been kept on after I went to Ticehurst and it was Peter's full time job anyway. I didn't see much of them because I didn't need looking after. I did go to Brighton Hospital for a bit of extra physio. Grant arranged for us to have a try at scuba diving to which we all agreed. We all got in the water different ways, but we found it better to get into the water before putting the apparatus on our backs.

I found it quite difficult to keep straight because the apparatus kept pulling me down. I had a weak side, a damaged left arm and terrible balance. That was my first and last time scuba diving. All the lads met in the bar and it was easy access because the bar was near the pool and upstairs. You see men can go there for some training or just for a holiday. We got on well with some of the old guys.

CHAPTER 3

Veterans' Stories

I myself have a lot of respect for the old veterans, what they achieved was nothing short of a miracle and that's why we are free and don't let anybody ever forget World War II. The old guys are great and what they achieved is re-enacted in films. One such man is Ray Sheriff who was injured in 1944 by a 88 Mortar bomb and as a result is totally blind.

He was actually at the Battle of Arnhem, which was portrayed into the great movie, *A Bridge Too Far.*

Ray speaks about Arnhem: Operation Market Garden.

We didn't know where we were going until a few days before. Our Para were fortunate with the landing and as a result were unopposed. Fortunately the majority of us didn't come into serious contact with the enemy until we were four miles away from the objective.

My old Regiment the Ox and Bucks were actually used as Glider Troops and they had a difficult job landing in gliders. We all went through a hell of a time.

In the first three days of battle we lost nearly 75% of the men either dead or injured. The only time I had to cross the river was in the planes but we were surrounded and were driven into small pockets and then Jerry would give us a hammering. Col Frost and 2 Para did extremely well and held the bridge on their own with no other support for approximately four days until they were finally overrun. They were engaged in some of the bitterest and fiercest fighting of the battle. There was an SS Panzer Division doing an overhaul in the woods when we came down. I think they were resting and re-fitting their tanks for some unknown battle but they went quickly into action when we landed.

We didn't find out till after the War that the Germans knew we were coming and consequently were waiting for us. We only had light carriers and of course small arms and 25 pounders, but these were no match for the German Panzers. So we were in a losing battle straight from the Drop Zone. There had been a leak in security. The Germans knew we were coming but I don't think the Panzers were stationed there deliberately. They were simply doing an overhaul and taking time out from the war.

Our objective was the bridge and we landed about eight miles away. This was very good planning because we couldn't very well land directly on the bridge as this would have been a complete and utter shambles. Operation Market Garden was designed to shorten World War II by six months but sadly the mission was termed a failure because there was so much resistance from the enemy and as a result we had a high degree of casualties, so it did not shorten the war. We were only two miles from the DZ but we couldn't get through the massed ranks of the Germans. I was hit by an 88 mm bomb and have been totally blind for the past 58 years, ever since the shrapnel from the bomb went into my eyes. I was then taken into a Dutch house and placed in a cellar.

Over the next three days they were trying to get

us in to the hospital at Arnhem and they had a number of Red Cross jeeps available. It was on one of these Jeeps that I was actually shot in the leg. They didn't stop firing even if God himself had been strolling across the battlefield.

After the Battle of Arnhem I was taken prisoner and transported into Germany where I remained for the remainder of the war. It was only about six months. In 1945 when the war ended we all came home and I was admitted into Stoke Mandeville where St Dunstans had two or three wards. From there I went to Church Stretton and trained as a tobacconist and consequently St Dunstans loaned me the money to start a tobacconist business, Well I was in this line of employment for 12 years. I really enjoyed the profession so I bought the business from St Dunstans. Then I went training at Ovingdean, St Dunstans as a telephonist and I worked for an engineering firm for 20 years.

I started raising money for charity in 1955 but this was mainly through swimming. I was participating in running events, all for sponsorship, and I did that right up until 1990 also I used to run marathons about one a year. What an achievement, raising money for 35 years, but that's not all. I started parachute jumping as a blind person and up to the present date I have raised over £13,000 for various charities. In 1990 I started going back to Arnhem every 17 September to jump on the actual LZ we parachuted on to in 1944. I have jumped about 30 times altogether and that includes my Military jumps. I jump tandem now which is far more exciting as you get a excellent thrill. When you are up at 12,000 feet you start to get a bit anxious for your tandem

Ray with his tandem master

master because he's probably never jumped with a blind person before. Well when we were jumping in the war we had to jump at a much lower altitude to enable us to hit the ground quickly and hence, reduce the risk of being a slow moving target. The idea was to hit the ground in the fastest way possible. Well you couldn't very well go back up unless you were Superman.

I originally joined the Army in 1937 at the young age of 16. I volunteered for Special Training with the Paras in 1943. I gained my Para Wings after I completed 8 jumps from Whitley Bombers, and also two jumps from a cradle attached to Barrage Balloons from 800 ft. Also I was a founder member of 3 Para Battalion. In 1942 the Battalion was drafted into North Africa. Sadly I was wounded during fighting in the hills of Tunisia. Then we dropped into Sicily and into Italy, there was no combat necessary because they could run. In 1943 I returned to the UK to prepare for the 2nd Front dropped into Arnhem, Holland, 17 September 1944 and as a direct result was blinded by an 88mm mortar bomb. Thus I was taken prisoner and found myself going to North Germany, Stalag 11B. We were liberated April 1945.

This concludes Ray's story. He now lives with his wife Betty at Ovingdean. He does attend the house for swimming and for holidays as we all do.

One day I was stopped in my tracks by Christine the Training Officer and she informed me I was to be presented with a Gulf War Medal for my involvement in the Campaign, the very next day. At last something to show for nearly being six feet under. The rest of the day, I was involved in various lessons – it was certainly like being back at school.

That night Peter assisted me to get my Blues (uniform) squared away. All the fluff was taken from my Blues by using sellotape and you could use your hob nailed boots as a mirror, they were like a piece of glass after they were cleaned. The next morning I was woken early and quickly got myself shaved because I could always do that. In fact I didn't need much assistance at all getting into my Blues. It was great, all the heads of the various topics were present, and Col Bray. My parents had come down South especially and of course Peter and Lance were available.

I was amazed to see that General Keils was the officer presenting the medal. He had apparently asked to come and give me my medal because he had a lot of admiration and respect for me. He was the exact same officer who had presented my St Dunstans badge. Well you see I had been most seriously injured and I needed all the support

Steve down south with his proud Mam and Dad after
receiving his Gulf war medal

I could receive. I did feel very proud and rightly so, I
don't think it was for this reason. More likely it was
because I was a Royal Marine and he was extremely
proud of me.

There was a photo session, and as I write this
manuscript I cast my mind back to that particular day
and a small tear drops from my eyelash. When I remember
someone who is no longer with us. My mother. She was
so proud of me; well, she had seen me a wrangled, twisted
and bloody mess. It was a day to remember and cherish
for the rest of my life.

Col Bray asked us to collect in as many sponsors as
possible for St Dunstans because the Royal Marines were
going to participate in a wheelchair push from Brighton
to Eastney Barracks to meet Major General Keils at the
end. It would be a damned good effort.

Three Royal Marines came down south from
Newcastle. They were all pretty switched on (Good at

Steve with Jimmy, who performed the emergency tracheotomy

their jobs), but one was exceptional, and he was from RMR Tyne. Every Marine should be switched on. It is not essential but it helps a bloody lot. Steve was a driver, parachutist, coxan and he was AWT (Arctic Warfare Trained). Of course you first had to achieve your Green Beret and as we all know that is extremely difficult. We all set off and there was a whole crowd of us. The girls with us had the buckets out collecting money for St Dunstans and Grant was going to put the majority towards refitting the gym out with air pressure machines. The first two people we saw were Chris Eubank and his trainer. He was apparently in training for some future fight.

It was a walk in the park for me and the four Royal Marines using wheelchairs. Well obviously, we had nothing to do! But it must have been hard work for the Royal Marines pushing. 'Not really,' Steve said, 'we're all exceptionally fit Royal Marines.' It was over 60 miles and it was pretty tough. People were generous and including the sponsorship we collected a tidy figure.

We stopped at Bognor Regis for the night as this was about the half way point. The girls collected quite a tremendous amount of money for the cause. All of a sudden everyone was in the bar. It was quite a sight all of us packed into the bar area. Col Bray was enjoying himself as he always did on such occasions. Some of the lads got pissed, no names mentioned but they were entitled to. There was a Royal Marine from the Corps assisting us. He was attached to RMR Tyne and he apparently was a good egg (i.e. somebody who is well liked and can be relied upon, would do anything for his mates). We all had breakfast which was very important, especially for the Royal Marines pushing the wheelchairs.

Races were taking place on route but I didn't win any because of my arm. It looked normal, but what is normal? Now it is fine. The only problem I have is when I pick up a cup it tends to shake, but only occasionally. I have no co-ordination and it does get on my tits. Well it would be untrue to say I have none, only a small fraction is correct. We continued on and all the cars passing by were tooting their horns to show their support. Some of them even stopped to hand over donations by placing money in the girls' buckets. Good skills, girls!

The big statue which stands at Eastney Barracks outside the Royal Marines Museum was standing proudly to attention as a mangled crowd rushed by. This statue is a piece of history as it commemorates the now famous yomp the Royal Marine Commandos were involved in during the Falklands Campaign. General Keils and the CO from our Unit were present, and handing out screams of encouragement.

Ironically the Commanding Officer from our Unit had

been Steve Spark's Commanding Officer down the Falklands War. It just shows how small and special the Marine Corps actually are, a lot of lads know each other.

Steve Sparks speaks about the Falklands War:

I joined the Royal Marine Commandos in 1980 and I passed out of training in July 1980. I first saw service abroad in 1981 where I achieved the Arctic Warfare Qualification in Arctic Norway. All of a sudden we were at war with Argentina. Our CO informed us as part of 42 Cdo we were to deploy to the Falklands to expel the intruder with 3Cdo Bde. We didn't have a troop ship that was adaptable enough to transport all the men and equipment the journey down south so actually we had to use the cruiser Canberra as a troop ship. We all thought the whole conflict would be over when the bulk of us arrived. We never dreamed we would actually have to fight.

We kept practising our military skills by firing our weapons off the back of the ship and participating in various command tasks. We would take turns with other units at running round the promenade. This was the middle part of the ship and we would have an extremely ball bagging time. We were running with full kit and various section weapons. All the various units had a designated slot in the day to practise and train. As time progressed we received reports from the UK that we were going to war. It was just like deploying to Arctic Norway, which is where the Royal Marines train every year. We didn't treat it any different from a routine Exercise. We did exactly what we were taught in training; all of our drills just slipped into place. Above all we are extremely Professional.

When we arrived we were subjected to quite a bombardment from the Argentine Air Force, who were very skilful, unlike their Army. They were very frightening and they hit a number of ships. The spirits of the men were high and we all wanted to kick the invader off the islands. We all thought how dare the Bastards. The landings were almost unopposed, but sadly we still received a barrage from a different array of weapons. We all landed at separate intervals. The Argentine Force was mostly made up of conscripts and some of them ran away but they had regular forces as well and they proved a tough nut to crack.

We all had separate objectives and the main reason the Parachute Regiment got to Port Stanley before Royal was simple. That in their haste to beat the Royal Marines they ran through minefields and consequently they suffered casualties. Old Royal just took their time and carried out the correct procedures and drills. Not taking anything away from the Paras but if I had to go to war again, I know who I would rather be fighting alongside. Not much chance of that taking place as I suffered a diving accident and as a direct result was medically discharged.

When we finally marched into Stanley, the place was a complete shambles. Over the next few months there would be a tremendous amount of clearing up to be done. It just shows the difference between a professional force and a band of poorly trained conscripts. Let this be a lesson to any other dictator who attempts to overrun our proud island, or any of its Sovereign countries by means of force.

CHAPTER 4

Memories and Travels

One of the lads kept broadcasting how good RAF Hedley Court was! So I asked Col Bray if he could get me in, to which he agreed. It was difficult because I was discharged from the Corps. The MOD had kept me in the Corps until my War Pension had come through because I had been serving with them and was actually signed up with 3 Cdo (Commando) Brigade. I think Major General Keils had a small say in the matter. Quite a few of us youngsters were leaving including me but I wasn't travelling home. This time I was driven to the Rehabilitation Centre at RAF Hedley Court.

It was made up from occupants from the three services, all present for their separate reasons. It was pretty peculiar but there was a guy from Steve Pendleton's regiment the Royal Green Jackets. They called him Ned the Med and he was a right character, as the majority are in HM Forces. Another guy was present and I shared a Grot (Room) with him along with two other guys. He had been in the Para Regiment. This was a mistake putting me next to him, because he was already there, it was his territory, plus Royal Marines and Paras are not meant to get along, but we got on fine. It's not really true what you hear about Marines and Paras it's only banter. Well that's certainly true with the older ranks but I'm not so sure about the new recruits. It was exactly how I'd perceived it, just like a boot camp of the type I'd seen in the United States of America.

That night I drifted off to sleep, thinking and dreaming of my trip to America; training with the US Marines and thinking of Boot Camps or Training Camps. Well I had received quite a good recommendation from the Unit to enable me to go. A Captain, a Cpl and me as a humble Marine were selected to attend a course prescribed by the 4th Recon (Reconnaissance) United States Marines. It was to be held at Texas. We all arrived at the Unit in good time to get an early start and miss the traffic around Newcastle. Captain Robinson drove the hired car first and then Gary and me drove next because we all had clean Driving Licences. Eventually we arrived but the traffic had been horrendous.

We stayed the night at RAF Brize Norton and drove up to a civilian airport and flew out to the United States that way. When we arrived we met all the Americans and there was one Marine who was horribly burnt and he informed us that he was in the chopper crash in Libya, when they had attempted to save the American hostages. We all had a barbecue and got acquainted. There were plenty of nurses to get into but I was happily seeing Nicola, who was the mother of my daughter, Lindsey Adele, and anyway I was busy getting pissed. We stayed in Fort Sam in these wooden huts. The trucks would come and pick us up for the day's excursion and we were firing an assortment of weapons – everything from a Saw Anti Tank Rocket to a M16 Assault Rifle, and we were laying mines. Well we were all tasked to lay a Claymore (Anti Personel Mine) There was a knack to it, it was quite simple as long as you adopted caution.

We also did a Recce (Reconnaissance) patrol in a desert

Steve and the lads in Texas

area and through a series of rivers. A switched on guy who had been trained as a scout on the Mexican border led us. He was showing us how to search for traces of the enemy by pointing out how a footprint or a loose boulder, some trampled down shrub or some disturbed foliage were all telltale signs that would give away your position to the enemy. This was all revision because we had been shown before, but practice makes perfect. When we returned to the Camp everyone scrambled for the PX, this was equivalent to our NAAFI, which stands for Navy Army Air Force Institute.

We all picked up Aviator, American Pilots Glasses and as a result all thought we were Tom Cruise out of *Top Gun*, but we all stayed focussed. He is just a Hollywood film star and we were all quite professional.

We got our kit ready and we were all loaded onto a selection of buses. We arrived near to San Antonio, Texas at this camp on the beach with barbed wire round. Gary and I just looked at each other and shook our heads. We were supposed to train in this heat! I could cope with the heat, it was all the skirt watching us, but sadly when we started training they all moved away. The tents stood firm, the weather was amazing. We didn't unpack our Bergan (Rucksacks), you just lived out of them. This was the normal procedure in the Forces.

Training started with MREs (Meals Ready to Eat). This was very similar to our Rat Packs but tasted like shit. The heads (toilets) smelt like a fish wife's armpit. They were in a portacabin, and as you can imagine it bloody stunk. It was normal – a bit of shit didn't hurt a soul. We all fell into two ranks, but the heat was terrific. I thought I was in a furnace and I kept saying to Gary, 'I'm going to dive in the Ocean in a minute,' but Gary wouldn't allow me to as he was in charge. Gary was one of the Physical Training Instructors at our Unit. All the Americans were hanging out, basically they were completely wrecked; I was fine. They obviously didn't receive the same hard training as our lads. I was the fittest there and with Captain Robinson looking on I felt so proud for myself and Royal.

Then we were tasked to swim out for about half a mile and then dive down and measure the depth of the water at low and high tide. This piece of work was called a Hydrographic Survey. We also had to test the ocean bed to enable us to see where was most suitable for a beach landing. We all got pissed again that night and even managed a bit of dancing. It was a regular occurence for the lads. It was a way to unwind after an incredibly ball bagging day.

The very next day we were again wet but this time we were having a race. Two Geminis were brought forward (these are like inflatable small boats that you can attach a motor to), but we were just using our arm power and it was extremely rough. The sun spilled out a brilliant glare and the ocean was as still as a line of statues just waiting for some inspection that would never take place. The race got under way and our boat was really going for gold. It was made up of occupants from the Americans, myself and Gary.

We all rowed so hard the veins in our arms were pumped up, you would think we had all been training in Gold's Gym with Stallone. We were certainly ripped, as the expression goes. The boats were neck to neck with water splashing and dripping from our faces. We were just edging in front when suddenly we hit the ocean bed and shingle, that signalled we had hit the shore and the end. Our boat had won by a small margin but it was the fun of taking part that counted. Still there's nothing wrong with a bit healthy competition. Marines thrive on it.

My head was spinning when I woke, I thought it had been stamped on. We had these wash basins in a cubicle. You had cleaning ladies, this was unheard of when I was in the Royal Marines, but I suppose it **was** a hospital. There was a bar that every man and his dog attended, it was just One Big Piss Up and I got pissed along with them. Well I was walking with two sticks; I just thought bollocks to this. Dave the physiotherapist was a good bloke so I asked him if I could give it a try solo, to which he agreed. I was walking about falling and hanging onto the walls and I would try to hurry so nobody would see me but sadly I was caught out and as a result was given my sticks back. So all that extremely hard work and I was still on two sticks. I was pretty pissed off. No, I was completely fucked off and I began to have my doubts as to whether or not I would ever walk again independently.

Of course I was already walking but it wasn't good enough for me and it wasn't good enough for my Mam. Well I was only admitted for an assessment and actually only there for a short period. I had come from the Jaws of Death and I wasn't going to give in now, not even if it put me back in a bloody coma. A short time passed and I was discharged from Hedley Court and actually returned to St Dunstans to continue with my rehabilitation. My life had changed and all because of a God damned truck. I was well and truly pissed off because I wanted to go home to oversee the construction of my bungalow, but instead I found myself returning to the House (St Dunstans). Not that it was horrible there but I just wanted to see the bungalow they were building for me. Have you ever tried to hurry up construction workers? I was itching to get my own opinion of the fabulous bungalow.

We arrived back at the House and I was surprised to see the majority of the trainees, as they were called, had left and only Steve Sparks, the lad who was a former Royal Marine and who had lost part of his sight in mysterious circumstances was left. Col Bray organized a trip to France; this was before the Channel Tunnel was built. So all of the gang had to travel by ship and consequently via the North Sea and the Channel. We caught the ferry early one morning and almost immediately everyone was crowding into the bar area. You wouldn't believe me if I said I didn't drink much, it was only because of the life threatening experience I had to contend with. Some bright spark told a hilarious joke and as a result I nearly fell down the bloody stairs in hysterics.

We all disembarked at France and quickly disappeared into the various cafes and of course bars. The time flew and in no time, we found ourselves rushing back to the terminal. Col Bray came along and stated that we had only fifteen minutes until the ferry returned so if we wanted any Duty Frees we had best be quicker than Roger Banister. After that, as you could imagine, it was one big mad dash. I must mention the items we brought back, especially the alcohol, were only used for our own consumption.

The ferry arrived back and we all disembarked and climbed aboard the waiting transport to carry us back to the house. We all had a superb time. Well, I had not visited France before, but I have been twice since I was down the South of England.

Let me explain. The first time I went for a holiday to France was when I took my ex girlfriend who used to live with me, for Valentines Day. She is called Nikki, short for Nicola. Not to get this girl confused with my daughter's mother who is also called Nicola. I wanted to do something special for a girl whom I definitely cared about and I still do but only as a friend now. We flew out of Newcastle and we stopped at Southampton and then progressed to Paris, through Charles de Gaulle Airport. Once inside the terminal building we looked around for special assistance, which helps you to and from the aircraft. Luckily we had received some help, otherwise we would have never found the exit. It was as hard as escaping from Colditz. But then what would I know, I wasn't there. Very few service men were actually imprisoned there; it was only used for RAF prisoners.

Finally we came outside and flagged down a waiting taxi. We got out near the Eiffel Tower and we checked in. One very small fact that became apparent is they wanted money for transporting the APC (Armoured Personnel Carrier), another name given to the wheelchair by the lads of the UK.

We visited all the sites and even took a trip down the

River Seine. There was only one problem – the weather was really disgusting and it pissed down. Well it was February and it was the wrong time of year for the climate to be in the 100s. One day we were out for a stroll and this frantic guy came up pointing to his camera. I thought he was going to attempt to mug us but all he wanted was to take our photograph. We allowed him but I didn't realize we had to pay for the privilege. I was a bit slow. I thought he wanted a memory of France. I said to Nikki we have just been conned.

We went down the Champs Elysées and we visited a tremendous amount of bars and cafes. We were being right spotters looking at museums and historical buildings, but I had to do what the woman said. You know what I mean, Lads? To name just a few of these sights – The Arc de Triomphe and the Louvre. We even went up the Eiffel Tower. Well you couldn't say you had been to Paris and not been up the Eiffel Tower. It was only a short break and the weather was appalling, especially that boat trip down the River Seine.

We travelled back to the UK via Southampton and then up the country to Newcastle Airport where we were met by Bob of Westborne Taxis. Taking us to the airport had been Bluey, they are both local lads. Occasionally I travel up to the local watering hole and have a drink with Bluey and Sandra. The pub is a popular venue, named Tinker's after the previous landlord.

One time when I was at St Dunstans I met a French girl who was working at the House. She was assisting with the old veterans' care. We made friends and I took her out quite frequently when I was there for a holiday or some training on the computers or in the gym. I attended quite frequently when I was training for the London to Brighton Bike Ride.

One night we went to the pubs of Brighton. Carine loved the pubs because there was nothing like them in France. It was ironic really, all she drank was soft drinks. I was only there for two weeks but I made a vow to keep in touch when she returned to France and left St Dunstans.

As a result of us being friends I was invited over to France, to stay at her parents' house. I flew exactly the same route as I had taken with Nikki, but at Paris I changed planes and flew on to Strasbourg. I was met by Carine and her father who owned a factory, and was driven a long way to a quiet village with a large house. Carine took me to see what was left of the Maginot line and we went to see a cottage that the family owned. It was close by and I think it belonged to Carine's grandparents.

In France they have a different way of life from us. For example, not many of them go out to friends or relatives, they all go to bed early. This is something we should all practise. It is amazing that just over the channel a totally different lifestyle exists. They don't seem bothered about exercise like we are in this country. Well the family did have an indoor swimming pool but their idea of swimming was certainly different to the English way, it was sitting about the pool relaxing, but in their defence it was a small pool. Of course, lots of Englishmen are fat and do sit around the pool surveying the women, we all do, but I exercise as well.

All the family lived in three houses joined together; they were more like flats.

I did challenge the brother to a game of chess, which I won, but he won the second encounter. He was a very skilful player. We visited a forest area near to the bunkers used by the French to defend against raiding Germans during World War II. I only knew a very small amount of French so I found it a bit difficult. Well, I should have studied at school instead of playing the fool. I would advise anybody who is making the short journey over the channel to learn a little bit of French. All the various airport handlers asked if you spoke French and when you said just a fraction, they were not impressed. It will probably all change when they read this book!

Then I said my farewells and Carine and her father accompanied me to Strasbourg Airport. Once there, I again said Au revoir and then I was on my way via Paris. Back to what I choose to call God's country, but then everyone assumes they come from God's Country. A peculiar turn of events and I found myself sitting all alone in a compartment separated by a curtain. I signalled to the host and asked why this was. He informed me that my ticket had been Second Class and they had put me in there because they had guessed, wrongly of course, that I needed more room. I thought to myself cheeky bastards, talk about discrimination. To them I am exactly the same as everyone else only I have been unlucky. I have girlfriends just the same as any other guy. The majority of the population thinks that you should be locked up. They don't want to be seen associating with you and if you ask them questions they seem to want to escape quickly. So fuck if I speak slowly, it's better than not speaking at all. The people who know me understand and what's more the females know exactly what I mean. I don't have to remind you, three quarters of the world would have surely perished or would have been a vegetable if they had to contend with what I had been through. I am extremely fit. Always have been and always will be.

Well that's why I'm alive. I do have quite a good life under the circumstances and have lots of good friends and a fair few acquaintances. Attending the gym at Springs

Tony and Steve at the Gym

is a weekly occurrence and there's a lot of good people always present. It was exactly the same as the two other gyms I trained at. Jim Morton is the gym Manager and his girlfriend works there too. She is called Christine and works in the bar. Jim is a good egg. I used to train with a lad called Steve Watson but unfortunately he supports Liverpool. He left and took up a position at another gym but we kept in touch and he attended the Sunderland v Liverpool game with me, disastrously we got beat! The very next encounter, when we played them at the Stadium, incredibly we beat them by the exact same score 2 – 1. Supporting Sunderland Association Football Club is a large part of my free time. My mate Tony says he could think of better ways to spend a Saturday, but that is only because he follows Newcastle and the Mags are flying high at present.

Miss F. Murray managed to progress my application for a parking space. She does a tremendous amount of work for the disabled and injured supporters, even organizing functions and arranging for us to meet the players.

My friend, Jim Dadswell and his daughter, Paula give me a lift to the match. I have gone to the match with Jim since Sunderland played at Roker Park. I did go down to Wembley in 1985 with Tommy B and some schoolmates but sadly we were beaten 1–0. When I was at school myself Big A and Mac the Knife used to go down to Roker Park to watch the G force (Marco Gabbiadini and Eric Gates, our two strikers). I certainly feel sorry for the Sunderland supporters because they have been forced to watch abysmal performances for far too long and I blame the previous Manager for not spending money when we were second in the table. The board know that if they are relegated, they will still have at the very least 25,000 fanatical diehard supporters following them around. Watching Sunderland is making me go grey. Well that's my excuse. Most Sunderland fans couldn't imagine us being in the top 6 of the premiership but that's where we should be aiming at and that's where we belong. Unfortunately the Club doesn't share the same ambition as the fans. Of course that's only my opinion, but we are an enormous club.

I was only back at the House a very short time, then I returned home to the Northeast. St Dunstans are very good because they assist with travel arrangements backwards and forwards. I had to stay with my parents until the bungalow was constructed, which was approximately three weeks.

One day at the completion of the bungalow, I went down to the vicinity of the building site and gave the workers some alcohol as a small gesture to show my appreciation.

It was fabulous when I actually moved in. It was very spacious inside and had Delft Rails in the hallway, three bedrooms, a study, kitchen, living room and a garage. It was tucked away in a small cul-de-sac. It is fantastic to know that St Dunstans is out there if you have to contend with an unfortunate episode in your life.

My parents were also a good help. Sadly my Mother has now passed away and my Dad is attending kidney dialysis and he can only visit when he gets a lift from my younger brother and we go out for meals etc. My uncles live close by and they are a good help with various aspects of my extremely busy life. When he was well, my Dad was always coming up with these bright and wonderful ideas. This particular day he suggested that I go Adventure Training at the Calvert Trust. This is situated at Kielder in Northumberland near to where I live. I had some free time, so I decided to go. All sorts of people were admitted there for various reasons. I didn't even attempt to get help with the price as I had a War Pension. I enjoyed the abseiling, I was at home with that activity, but unfortunately I struggled with the climbing due to my injury.

Next it was the archery and I was quite a good shot. I don't know why I'm not even considered for the St Dunstans Team, after all I was a good shot, but I think that's what they are afraid of. I did spend quite a long period of time establishing a tight group in the centre of the target the Gold – unlike darts, the centre of the target is not called the bull, but the Gold.

We did a spot of sailing. And now they have got a series of ropes called the Zip Wire, but there's that much emphasis on safety, you hardly move. The Death Slide at the Commando Training centre does resemble it a little but only a little. It is far more extreme, but this one is designed for people with injuries. Also they have horse riding, and you can take part in a small orienteering exercise. It would have been simple if I could see the bloody map but I had problems making out the fine detail.

On the way back home I gazed out of the window and suddenly realized where we were. Because the Forces use the area as a Training Camp quite frequently they blow the shit out of that area all the time.

The very first time I travelled to Kielder I was with the Cubs, and I had a ball of a time. The next occasion I was taking part in a T-Company exercise, the whole Royal Marine Reserve.

I visited Catterick when I was with the Royal Marines and we were practising FIBUA, which stands for Fighting in Built up Areas. You always worked in pairs, hence your 'Oppo' (Buddy) and he always covered you. When you were clearing a room, the Number 1 throws in the grenade and then you wait approximately 7 seconds and then the Numbers 2, 3 and 4 rush in and begin clearing the building. All you could see were tank tracks as far as the eye could see. It was always raining every time you went away, we got used to the filthy weather. The lads would just look and say 'Typical of the UK, always fucking raining.'

We were all pretty experienced by this time in our role. Continuation training carried on and I first saw service abroad on Ex Hairspring, this took place in Norway. The

Steve at Otterburn with Cpl Rennie

role of the Royal Marines is to guard NATO's northern flank. At least it was when I was serving! I presume it's all changed now. Travelling to Norway was an annual and essential part of life as a Royal Marine. This was because of all the skills we learned and the experience gained and because the Royal Marines are experts in mountainous terrain and cold weather conditions. Before anyone could go to Norway they had to learn to cross-country ski, which was bloody ball bagging, more so carrying 100 pounds of various items of kit. Hence we went to Arbroath to learn. We were taught by an MSI (Mountain Ski Instructor), and this took place at 45 Cdo Royal Marines in Scotland. Our instructor was a really experienced and switched on soldier. He was in the SBS (Special Boat Service).

The most essential part of cross-country skiing is being able to stop and to balance. Like the majority of tasks, the rest comes with a lot of practice. Immediately we were taught how to stop the easiest way, which was the Snow Plough stop. I am only speaking individually because there were a lot of experienced skiers in the Royal Marines but in Norway it was a nightmare trying to stop with a massive Bergan, equipment and a weapon attached to your body. Well over 100 pounds is carried by every Royal Marine in Norway and trying to ski with all that baggage on your back is certainly no picnic. You soon get the hang of it but if not a lot of precious energy is wasted getting back to your feet when you fall over, not to mention probably giving your position away to a watching enemy. We were taught how to turn by way of a Snow Plough Turn. All the lads got some valuable practice in and after getting pissed every night all of the lads returned to the Northeast.

Before travelling to Norway a lot more emphasis on skiing was needed, so we went to a civi (civilian) ski slope just to become accustomed again. At the Unit a tremendous amount of work was taking place. All the stores were loaded into Shake-ons (large storage containers). All the Arctic Rat Packs (Rations), Weapons, Ammunition, Arctic Clothing, Ski Poles and of course the Pussi's Planks (a name given to the Skis by the Royal Marines of the UK). Then we flew courtesy of the Crab Fats (RAF) direct to Arctic Norway.

Back at home, just trying to live alone is extremely hard. Having only limited balance, one thing I find difficult is carrying a coffee from my kitchen to my living room without spilling any liquid. I have a home help to clean the house but with all the cutbacks in Social Services they can only spare once a week, but I do get one hour's ironing. To this day I still struggle on but my friend Tony assists when we go swimming and to the gym. Actually I am his Personal Trainer. So I'm to blame when you see the state of him. He has a job. Music is his game and Tony is his name. Apparently he works as a DJ somewhere in Newcastle.

My Two Uncles are a fantastic help, Rosco is the scran man and Ned works too damn hard but he is always available to assist when necessary and he has been present since my family were at school.

But there are limitations. A minority of people, especially the older generation are not educated towards injuries and slight disabilities. Can you blame them? When they were young all the benefits probably were not available and they haven't come across anyone who is so determined to succeed where others have failed. I reckon there's a bit of the Marine still in me.

For example: a mate and I went swimming. The response I got was pathetic. People think they are helping but in fact they are not. They really make you feel incapable, and when they saw me swimming this old woman said 'eeh ... Can he swim? eeh bless him!' looking directly at my mate. This gets on my tits. I fully realize and understand that they think that they are helping but it makes you feel abnormal and it makes you feel like a little worm. Well to say I don't get frustrated and very pissed off would be untrue. I know most people at the pool but it's just these people who haven't come into contact with any human being who has a slight problem with their mobility. It's like that the world over. The exact same pathetic thing occurs. When you go into a shop, just because I use a cane (at present), so fuck, it doesn't mean I will always need it, especially if there is any skirt in the vicinity. I do go into a selection of stores where the staff know me and it doesn't present a problem. Well I'm just bringing it to the attention of society. Able-bodied people might think what the fuck is he talking about? But ask any injured person! Exactly the same applies if you go into a restaurant or café. 'Does he take sugar, does he want a straw? Is he alright?' Well, why not ask me? They wouldn't be like that if you didn't have a cane, unless they were on the moon. They always speak to the person assisting you. They do think they are helping you but it is so patronizing and so pathetic. Some people bend over backwards and that makes you embarrassed, especially when they do a sickly grin. The majority of the time it is fine but I get so frustrated. Why not treat me exactly the same way as other members of society? After all I only walk with a cane.

The young people of the world would agree but like I said I'm not getting at the older generation, it is just that they are not educated in the way of injuries or disabilities. Writing this book independently and carrying out the interviews personally, proves I am pretty intelligent.

It's totally different at Springs Health and Fitness Club. I don't get patronized. Is it my fault I got injured? At the end of the day, I was injured serving the UK.

My condition is definitely improving, if I compare it to when I was first injured.

Well I don't class myself as disabled for the simple reason that I do more rigorous training and activities than the average man.

CHAPTER 5

The Bike Ride

Dreaming one night, I realized that I wanted to fulfil a challenge that I had always dreamt about completing. I dreamt of whizzing through the air at a rapid rate of knots, but sadly because my mobility problems were improving I had no intention of breaking a leg parachuting, so I had to decline. So I asked Grant to come up with some suggestions. St Dunstans always entered a team in the London Marathon and the London Bike Ride. I couldn't very well run in my condition, so doing the 55-Miles on a suitable bike seemed the most efficient way to get from London to Brighton. As a direct result parachuting was out of the question.

Training started almost immediately and St D's was at hand to assist as they always were. As soon as I decided that I wanted to participate, my static exercise bike was ordered and training commenced. I used to travel down to Brighton to train all the time flying, courtesy of British Airways.

This was the first bike we ever had and we completed the race on it. It was a strange looking contraption. An upright bike with 1 wheel at the front attached by a long pole to a sit down bike with 2 wheels at the back. This bike was called a Trike Conversion and we did get the piss taken out of us quite a bit. The Royal Marines assisting us were not impressed with the clowns taking the urine. Once, when I first started training, Grant and I took the bike to a park and were almost wiped out by

Grant and Steve on the first Bike Ride from London to Brighton.
Note Steve's Sunderland shirt.

a large vehicle. Afterwards, laughing about it, I just said
to Grant 'Not again'. We used to do a lot of hills because
Brighton is in an extremely hilly part of the country.

I myself put in some rigorous training and I was
extremely fit and ready for just about anything, especially
in my condition.

My mate Gary Lomas who was blown up defusing a mine in the Gulf War was also taking part in the bike ride. Gary does absolutely brilliant on his own, for most of the time and he still manages to beat most of Blackburn at pool. This is in spite of having only one eye with tunnel vision. He does pull the skirt; it must be his sunglasses.

My girlfriend at that time and myself went down South for the bike ride, but not before achieving a total of £7,000 sponsorship. The CGRM achieved an amazing amount with a little help from General Keils and the whole Corps collected a figure of £3,000. That included the fabulous RMR, and that proved a tall order, to actually have them separating from their hard earned pennies.

We set off early and travelled up to London. We squeezed through the massed ranks of people with their two-wheeled pushbikes. Sadly for the riders, it was the hottest day of the year and the tarmac was actually melting with the intense heat.

Disguised in the crowd and cheering me on was General Keils and the CGRM (Commanding General Royal Marines). A small contingent of Royal Marines was on hand to assist where necessary. What Grant didn't appreciate was the simple fact I had trained like a Trojan, primarily for the event, but I had not accounted for Killer Hill. This hill we had come into contact with, whilst training. It was a nightmare and would have been really simple to manage if I had been able bodied but unfortunately not.

As we set off, Grant informed me it was going to be a scorcher, 'Put plenty of sun cream on' he screamed, with his mouth full.

The team consisted of myself in tandem with Grant

Cooper and my mate Gary Lomas in tandem with the delightful Linda Stringer. Neil Swan of fundraising accompanied Grant and myself all the way round the course. The two lads from the Sports and Recreation Department, Mike Garden and Dave Goldsmith, were also present in the event. They were acting as back-up, but sadly they experienced problems of their own, due to distribution of weight. Also present were my old computer teacher, Janis Sharp and Paul her No 2. Also taking part were Trevor and Dave Vinall, and Mike Varney from Transport further strengthened the team.

It was quickly approaching midday and the heat was intense. It did turn out to be the hottest day of the Millennium. The going was tough and it was impossible to cycle up the ascents with a mass of people. Dehydration was high on the agenda.

The going was agonizingly slow. If it had been a clear run we would have completed the race in four hours but unfortunately 27,000 riders jammed us up. Lying sprawled out at a food and drink stop, the mobile rings and it is General Keils offering words of encouragement and informing me that there was only 48 miles to go. I just laughed and replied 'Cheers Sir, but I really didn't want to hear that.'

I said to Grant 'You could fry an egg on the road, it's so bloody hot.' I had this piss pot helmet on my head, so I asked Grant if I could take it off, but Grant replied 'Safety First!'

By the time we had gone 50 miles Grant knew every single item about Sunderland Association Football Club. He's probably forgotten about it now. We carried on as we were rapidly approaching Dichalin Beacon (Killer Hill). This hill carries on for almost a mile but it has a very steep incline.

A group of children were spraying the contestants down with water. When they saw my Sunderland strip I immediately received a full frontal jet of water, which I eagerly accepted. What made the matter worse was that they had someone on a loudspeaker, shouting at the top of his voice '500yds to Killer Hill.' Grant said he could do without that. When we arrived we were forced to queue. At the foot of Killer Hill the race marshals were actually sending up a handful of riders in separate intervals. The Royal Marines were on hand to assist when necessary, but I chose to cycle up with the minimum of support. I received a lot of stick, people shouting, 'He's not pedalling!', but you always get mindless morons all over the world. I think in their defence that they were just having a laugh at my expense.

The temperature was beginning to slacken but still a lot of people were going down because of the heat and a lot of riders were obviously suffering from dehydration.

Then at last we reached the top. After a long rest and a gallon of water, it was downhill and into Brighton. When we started to pick up speed Grant said, laughing, that it was the quickest we had gone all day. Then finally the Pavilion, the Palace Pier – 9 hours later, Endex !

It was a fantastic day at the end of July and that signalled to me that it was time for Summer Camp. Actually it was fully independent of St Dunstans and run by a delightful lady called Elspeth Grant. Chris Stilton spoke to me about the camp. He was my dog 'assistant' and his nickname is Chipper or whatever else I used to name him (but Chip mostly).

Well Steve, to the best of my knowledge the camp was started in 1951 and it was basically for blinded ex-service men. It really was a camp then and they lived in tents. There were ropes used as guide lines so the men could get to the mess decks and the Galley etc. When it did rain, which was often, being in the UK, it was like sleeping in a marsh. It was slippery and the grass turned into a mud bath. In those days the Duty Watch consisted of Naval Ratings from Seafield Park and female Wrens. The Naval Ratings were tasked to look after the men. Try to imagine, it wasn't a very comfortable holiday, just by the simple fact it was like living in a swamp.

I don't know how familiar you are with the field gun, but it used to feature in a tournament that took place at Earl's Court. The primary objective of the Field Gun Team was to manoeuvre a self-propelled gun over the obstacles in the shortest time possible and to reach the finish. We did attend the last ever Field Gun Tournament at Earl's Court and of course Royal was present, they were completing a serious of displays.

The Field Gun event was taking place at this time and a certain Field Gunner Trainer, who went by the name of Jock Scott, was the instigator of establishing the dogs for the St Dunstaners. It's a term of endearment that we are called dogs. E.g., we guide the men around onto ships and other mess decks and basically we assist where necessary. Most of the younger St Dunstaners are not totally blind but there a fair few who are. Most of the lads have what is known as tunnel vision. My eyes are definitely affected but some people would not claim I am visually impaired but then, they are not doctors.

The Camp used to be held at HMS Daedalus and the Field Gunners returning from Earl's Court used to be on hand to assist. The facilities at Daedalus *were fantastic. You had the runway, which could be used to accommodate a walking race, glider rides and for those St Dunstaners who wanted helicopter rides, but obviously not the younger guys as we used helicopters extensively during training. That is how the Field Gunners and Mr Scott got involved with St Dunstans. As far as I could make out the first introduction for St Dunstans and the Field Gun combined was in 1954. Chip said that date was approximate.*

At HMS Daedalus we used to be billeted in the PO's mess but used to use the Chief's mess for our entertainment. We would also go out for visits to various Armed Forces Museums. We also visited the Victory, Nelson's Flagship, then the Warrior, which was actually the first iron clad vessel. We were invited into the British Legion and the Conservative Club. We were also invited to join the Nurses at Haslow. When we turned up they put on a free bar and some scran (food) and that was superb. You are also invited into the wardroom for a night of entertainment and a quiz and of course free drinks. The night is always very well attended and subsequently enjoyed by all.

We participate in a games night, I think there's a bit of cheating going on but its just a daft laugh. That takes place in the PO's mess. This consists of skittles, golf and guessing what a certain object is and putting together a right-angled torch. All the St Dunstaners flourish in this competition. This torch is used by the Military and all St Dunstaners who are completely blind do complete this task very quickly and effectively. We all compete very admirably in all avenues of the games night.

As time changes the St Dunstaners get less and less.

Well we don't want any more casualties, especially any with eye injuries. Originally the camp was designed for the Ex Service men who lived in Brighton and the surrounding area to give the wives a break. Of course it is not like that now. Most of the men live independently when they are not pulling skirt.

My first experiences of working with St Dunstans were in 1973 at Daedalus. Of course we were very lucky there but now we are at HMS Sultan we have not got the space even though Sultan is a much bigger training establishment.

There is quite a substantial age bracket between the men from World War Two and the younger lads like you, Steve. Now the Field Gun is over we struggle to get the extra assistance.

Some people who assist are Marty Webb (Spider Webb) and his lovely wife, Trish. Marty is a former PTI in the Royal Navy and he plans the Sports Day. The sports consist of the shot, goal kicking, golf, basketball, walking race and various other sporting pursuits. Then you have Pete Westbrook and his wife Pat who assist where necessary. You also have Brigit who is a former nurse and takes care of all Medical needs whilst the camp is taking place. You have Brigit's daughter, the amazing Jenny and her incredibly small daughter who is apparently a teacher, Marie. She is very nice and assists all the lads. Not forgetting Brigit's great husband, Bill who did actually teach you to sing that song, Steve. It went something like this:

'Oh Lord its hard to be humble, when you're perfect in every way,

I can't wait to look in the mirror, cause I get better looking each day

65

To know me, is to love me, I must be a Hell of a Man.

Oh Lord its hard to be humble but I'm doing the best that I can.'

Then you have Former Field Gunner, Kevin Rickson who still thinks he's serving — he is so pussers it's unbelievable — and not forgetting his beautiful wife the great Yvonne who does help out.

Always present is Dave Burrows the mess President and taking over the St Dunstaners is an ace guy called Kirby. Also available are Al Price, Arnie Thompson and Ginge Gier. Arnie handles all aspects of transport. There is a perfect lady who assists all the men and she is quite experienced. Apparently she used to be a Wren and her name is Liz.

The sun was beating down but there was a fresh, cool breeze blowing me, Gary and Chip whilst we waited for the transport. A lady turned up, who we used to call Tadziki. A few years ago we kept going on about Tadziki which is a mixture of yoghurt, cucumber and garlic and it is extremely nice. Sadly Jean's recipe didn't seem to taste like the Greek version. With all due respect to Jean, 'She tried!'

The bus arrived and Kevin Rickson was shouting out orders. 'The bus is leaving in 5 minutes.' Most of the men were still upstairs but he kept on shouting and his shouts turned to screams.

Then I noticed a figure coming towards us at the same time as Karl, another young man joined us. As the figure became closer and into focus, I realized it was General Keils. He had obviously come down South to attend the Isle of Wight trip, which took place annually. What thrilled me more was the fact that he had come especially to be my personal guide.

Finally we were en route. We reached Whitehaven Ferry Terminal and everyone was ushered into the Terminal Building. General Keils was locked in conversation with Elspeth Grant.

On the ferry Jimmy Andrews, the ex-Field Gunner was dishing out tots of Pusse's Rum. It's tradition for men in the Navy and it was abolished 32 years ago but the custom is still carried out by Jimmy. He now is outside and currently works for the MOD Police. Me and the Lads think it's disgusting but Jimmy actually likes the stuff. To me it tastes like engine fuel and this is very scarey.

It was Cowes week and there were a tremendous variety of small crafts out in the sea. We arrived and went straight to our first rendezvous with alcohol in the British Legion. General Keils was causing quite a stir among the Ex-Veterans. We enjoyed a bag meal and two drinks. If you needed more beverages you paid. A various number of St Dunstaners, General Keils, Jenny, Trish, Gary, Chip and myself, and I nearly forgot the fantastic Marie – well she was that small I almost forgot about her – took part. We all enjoyed the glorious sunshine and as a result all had a craving for ice cream.

The group of us watched the amazing number of yachts floating along the currents. The time seemed to pass by at an incredible speed and soon it was time to climb on board for that relatively short journey back to the UK That same night we all attended a quiz in the wardroom and General Keils was in my team. Needless to say we didn't win!

While I was at Camp I had a quick chat with Gary Lomas. 'Well Gary when exactly did you join the Army?' I asked. Gary spoke briefly about the Army and the Gulf War.

I joined up with the Army in 1986 with the Royal Engineer's in Gibraltar Barracks, which is in Surrey. After I completed basic training, I moved to Kent to become a member of a Commando Troop. Every member must first pass the Commando Course and consequently achieve a Green Beret, which did in fact enable us to work alongside 3 Cdo Bde (3 Commando Brigade). We were an independent Cdo Trp within the BDE. Also I did complete a rigorous Diving Course and it was no picnic.

When I was on a well-deserved vacation as a civilian with my friend, we heard the news that suggested war was imminent. When we got back to Camp, we were informed that as part of 3 Cdo Brg, we were to be deployed to the Gulf region with the 7th Armoured Brg who had gone there as a fighting force to expel the intruder.

Our primary role was Bomb Disposal and we were deployed for that role with 3 Cdo Bde. We were in fact EOD, Explosive Ordinance Disposable, Clearance and Search. Our Trp did join up with the SBS (Special Boat Service) and were Part of the Liberation Team for the British Embassy in Kuwait.

In their haste to withdraw the onslaught of the Allies, the Iraqi Army left a dreadful array of booby traps and mines etc. All of the trenches were rigged up with booby traps, so we were tasked to deal with this little hiccup. We were ordered, as EOD Bomb Disposal to make safe all the defensive positions and also explode all the booby traps, mines, rockets, mortars and ammunition on sight in situ.

As the Campaign was approaching its close, whilst completing this task, I was closest to an exploding mine and lost my right eye completely. I also suffered

some facial injuries and received damage to my left
eye. I was loaded onto a chopper and flown to a
field hospital in Kuwait but sadly the treatment I
needed was far too extensive to be performed in a
field hospital. I was again flown by Chopper to
Riyadh, the capital of Saudi Arabia. Within 36 hours
I was loaded on a plane and flown back to the UK,
to a civilian facial injuries unit at Oxford, where I
woke up. I was horribly confused as you can
appreciate. Once there, I received the surgery I
desperately needed.

I first heard about St Dunstans when a Welfare
Worker came to see me and as you can imagine I
was terribly confused and disorientated but I did
assume it was something to do with a church. Due
to my own ignorance, I told her to piss off, I later
apologized.

I said to Gary 'It's fine, even General Keils hadn't heard
of it, and he's on the Council of St D's. Ironically he is
only on the Council since I was damaged by that 4-ton
truck.' Gary continued:

When I got home another Welfare Worker came to
my house and she explained about St D's.
Consequently I was invited down to Brighton for the
weekend and I stayed for 9 months. The training I
received was extremely beneficial and that is where
I met you Steve, at the training establishment at
Ovingdean, near to Brighton.

St Dunstans organize an activity weekend, which
all St Dunstaner's are invited to attend, if they are
prepared to exert themselves completing a various
array of pursuits, such as white water rafting, dry
slope skiing, rock-climbing, abseiling and canoeing –

69

these are just a handful of pursuits we find ourselves taking part in.

*Also we like to stress its about **ABILITY** AND NOT DISABILITY, AND WE CAN DO THAT!*

In all of these separate situations it's so important to challenge your blindness and challenge your own physical restrictions. It's very important that you don't lose touch with your skills or the things that you are able to do as this gives you a sense of achievement.

*St Dunstans also enters a team in the London Marathon and I myself have completed that event, and in the process, raising a very substantial sum of cash for St Dunstans. Also I have completed the London to Brighton with you, Steve. When we are at the end, again we like to stress **we can do that!** I am a fit guy and I like to go swimming and running, when I can get myself a guide. In all of these pursuits, it's actually being out there and achieving something that matters.*

'I don't have a carer as such but I do need a touch of assistance now and then,' I stated 'I need a driver more than a carer.' That's a pathetic word established by the Government. A small minority assumes you can't even perform the easiest of tasks in every day life. What people don't seem to understand is that anyone who's been in the forces will not lie down. No matter whatever has occurred to that individual, but especially if they wear a Green Beret. Gary continued: 'With reference to what we've been saying about ability and not disability, I have this closing statement, No matter what happens you can't take the Army, the Marine in your case Steve, out of a man, you still have the volcano, the fire, burning inside you.'

Every day just walking over to the mess Gary notices

an improvement in my mobility. Well it's harder for me to see the gains because I am with myself constantly. Every year I attend this Camp, I improve. My current physiotherapist is ranked 7th in the world. She informs me that in her professional opinion, weight training works for me but this is harmful and totally unacceptable according to the majority of British physiotherapists. They stated that I would never get out of the Monster. Fortunately for me, I proved them all wrong. Then we all parted company and were all on our separate routes to various places in the UK.

Paddy Shelley speaks with regard to my mobility and my painfully slow progress:

Steve was referred to me in April 1998 by a senior physiotherapist at Hunter's Moor Rehabilitation Centre where he had been attending physio and his primary problem was Ataxia. They also stated that Steve continued to attend a Gym for exercise purposes even though they had advised him against it.

The very first time he attended the practice he did arrive for a two hour appointment to ascertain his main problem, courtesy of his beautiful girlfriend. He was walking with a stick very precariously, with a lot of extension tone in his leg and back. At times he did have a lot of flexibility in his trunk and at times with key parts of his shoulders being pulled in; the left one more than the right. Stephen's main goal was to walk outside without the aid of a stick.

He manages the majority of tasks himself. Going out tends to still cause Stephen a problem because of uneven surfaces and he can't cross a road on his own. Fortunately he doesn't need to because he goes most places by car. He does not go on public transport without an escort. With regards to his mobility he walks with a very wide base and doesn't do hills.

The treatment plan at this time was to ascertain where his middle line was especially with his trunk and to work to decrease his increased tone, which was falling. Stephen came four times in 1988 courtesy of his girlfriend whom he has now split up from ...

The idea in the first year was really to establish that he could lie on a wide base and to actually accept the base and get stretched out and also to learn a minority of information about where his body was.

In 1999 the work we had been completing on his left leg was very much better. Then we started to free his upper limbs specifically to try and get an increase in his arms being out away from his body in order to challenge his trunk movement patterns. Stephen had a lot of selective control in that he can move all 4 limbs but the sequencing combined with the stability is the big problem, which is why he has tremendous tone with his feet pushing off the floor constantly.

Stephen attended the practice 6 times – that was in 1999. Again we were working to actually get him in line and his maintenance was only taking one hour, so that we could work primarily to get his trunk in the middle and allow his arms to free off.

So the main objective was to increase his trunk alignment but to get his arms away from his body and to try and concentrate on getting a smaller base of support without his feet constantly pushing on the ground. There was a considerable amount of work done on Stephen's feet so that they could take up the base of support and allow his feet to be able to get his heel down, with his back and pelvis in more of an extended posture.

Stephen attended for a total of 7 sessions in 2000 but unfortunately he split up with his girlfriend so he was forced to come with a friend who worked for Head Start, a Day Centre he used to attend called Headway. He sometimes came with a lad called Mark but he felt he was a bit advanced so he doesn't attend on a regular basis. Stephen was much straighter at this period and taking more risks and consequently falling over continuously. He was naturally much better but at a price, very often damaging his head, but Stephen felt this was a risk worth taking. There was still a lot of the session being taken up with maintenance but his left leg was much more stable and he could maintain midline.

We still had to stretch out his arms and legs but his balance was becoming much better. We still had a tremendous problem with flexion in his trunk but his breathing pattern was still a massive problem with regards to his balance. At this stage the treatment pattern concentrated very much on increasing his breathing patterns and also to work on his head and neck together with his feet being firmly on the floor and to allow him to breathe more easily.

Following an hour's maintenance in every session we then started doing a lot of very difficult postural sets in order to stretch Stephen's body out in very different patterns of movement.

The treatment pattern was focussed on his speech and head – in many of the sessions in 2001, of which he had 7. The biggest goal again was to maintain his stability to have a smaller base of support. He still had a considerable number of problems regarding his mobility. His rib cage was still rotated at many points and this is something we had to make Stephen aware of but to Stephen there wasn't much wrong because he could bench press 200 pounds.

The movement patterns carried out in each session were starting to increase, because in 1998 we could only complete one postural set but now a lot more success was being accomplished. Now we were carrying out a tremendous amount of postural sets e.g. side sitting, kneeling and walking outside over rough terrain. The sessions continued to work more on breathing, particularly to get Stephen's voice to sound better and bring out different tones. Some people did think he was drunk, that's only whilst speaking on a telephone. It certainly frustrates Stephen because he is definitely intelligent. Well he's written this story independently with the assistance of his computer. This will surprise everyone what knows him because he's not 17 or 18 now.

We were still struggling throughout 2001 to actually get his feet on the ground, and there were a number of sessions when Stephen was extremely tired due to the simple fact that he was doing far more. His trip to Oz had been the highlight of the year.

In the middle of 2001 we got Stephen to do more side sitting and over a plinth and much more floor work. This maintained his balance but also gave him more freedom to take his arms away from his body, which enabled him to have more control. One of the biggest problems we had was that he pulled forward because of tight structures around the anterior part of his chest, and this continued throughout 2001. In 2002 Stephen attended the practice 6 times but progress was pretty slow. He has still fallen a number of times primarily because he kept damaging himself by falling, especially walking outside wherever! By this time Tony was on the scene for transport.

The main goals this year have been neck and head alignment but Stephen has suffered a number of colds, which have obviously slowed him down. We want to actually increase his balance and try to increase his walking so that he doesn't fall so much. The last time Stephen came he managed to do a partial handstand and he had a much smaller base.

He has definitely improved and there is not so much emphasis on physiotherapy, which leaves more time to complete his book, 'Recovery from Hell'. Stephen has achieved great heights with every aspect of physiotherapy, far more than anyone predicted.

This concludes Paddy Shelley's story. I manage to walk inside without means of support but outside I prefer to use a cane.

I feel I am an inspiration to all because I will absolutely not give in.

CHAPTER 6

Arctic Training & More Biking

You could feel the temperature drop as the plane making a droning noise flew towards the Norwegian Coast. Soon we touched down with a screech of tyres. It felt extremely cold. The door was finally opened we all shivered with the intense temperature. One of the lads put the flaps of his Deputy Dog hat down in mockery. The correct name is just a winter hat. A working party was detailed to unload the stores. All the lads loaded on to the waiting transport and were driven off to the Camp, there to commence the extreme Cold Weather Training and the Novice Survival Course.

We all went out of the Grots (Rooms) and paraded in the Main Square. Soon the Blanket Stackers (Store men) handed out the ski poles and the Pusser's Planks. A day sack was required to carry a flask and whatever else you wanted to carry. You do lose a lot of energy and liquid is very important whilst working in the ARCTIC. You wear your windproof jacket with four large pockets and in the top left pocket a compass – very important for working in any environment; some waterproof matches and lighter, these are used for obvious reasons. Always carried is a FFD (First Field Dressing) in case of any casualties. The 2 remaining items carried in the top left-hand pocket are your snow goggles (Flies Eyes) a totally useless piece of kit but that's only my opinion!

Last you carry a facemask and this is used to protect the face against the elements of the fierce weather.

The contents of your bottom left pocket were as follows: A ski wax scraper used for scraping the old wax off your skis every time a new layer of snow had landed, and of course your ski waxes. Wristlets, these were a garment worn under your gloves, spare gloves and a candle. The candle was used to give light in the snow hole. There was a rota so everyone had a turn at Candle Watch.

The top right pocket held an Arctic Field Memoir; this was a useful piece of kit to have as when you are deployed in the field, it was essential to carry the correct contents in your windproof jacket pockets. These included, lip salve and a survival bag. In the bottom right it consisted of a head over and emergency rations.

Food is very important in the Arctic and a Trail Pack can be carried. This of course is optional. This is established using your own rations and can be eaten on the move. It enables you to eat small pieces often and it does keep up the reserves of energy. It consists of chocolate, glucose sweets, bits of biscuit, Dextral tablets and basically any other edible item you can get your hands on, but it's entirely up to the individual.

Our MSI (Mountain Ski Instructor) was a switched on guy and he was from our Unit. He was the same instructor who had taught us in Scotland.

The plain and simple fact is as follows: No man should attempt anything carried out in an Arctic environment, unless he understands the Arctic and carries the correct equipment. Well obviously you need to be super fit and it does help if you can ski.

'Today is skiing.' the instructor screamed. The ski training commenced. We did a tremendous amount of skiing and one of the lads picked up the courage and said

'If it's this hard without any kit, what's it going to be like trying to ski with a crate on your back?' (Nick-name for the Bergan).

We didn't find the answer to that small question until the first week's training was completed. What took place next was a serious of lectures on safety and that was very important whilst crossing ravines or gorges. You did take part in the fearsome ice training. What actually happened was a hole was made in the ice using a chain saw. You then manoeuvred your Bergan onto one of your shoulders, then one by one you ski into the hole and the murky cold water just hits you. You threw your weapon out first and then your Bergan. Your skis are lost under the ice and using your ski poles, you claw yourself out of the hole under your own steam. Then your oppos guide you into a ten man tent. If the marine is a complete Biff his Emergency Dry Clothing will be piss wet through, because you were informed to waterproof your Bergan. If so we have a problem.

After a short break back at the Norwegian Army Camp you are informed to fall in outside two Ranks with weapon, fighting order, day sack, snow shoes, your pusser's planks and of course your poles. The transport departed straight for the Training Area. We all alighted the transport and got our shit together.

First of all it was drilled into every Royal Marine just what the instructors wanted us to do. We had to do a series of 'ball bagging' section attacks. Running through the damned snow was hard enough without attacking an imaginary enemy. Just trying to accomplish a successful section attack wearing snowshoes is almost impossible but to Royal nothing is impossible! You also are instructed about Camouflage and Concealment, which is extremely difficult in the Arctic. You wear your Cam Whites

A cold place to stay for the night

Cammed out in Norway

Patrolling the icy roads

Being picked up by a chopper

(Camouflage) over your uniform and also you can wear a White Helmit Cover. White masking tape is fitted to your weapon and not your dick. A white cover would be used on your Bergan. Your fighting order could be dapped with spots of paint so to a passing plane it just looks like rocks. Another option is to paint your webbing entirely Then you go on exercise straight into the field (basically out, living and facing the ferocious weather.)

You live in ten-man tents and then you progress into four-man tents and then finally snow holes but remember whilst this is occurring a sentry must be on the look out, scanning the surrounding countryside, watching through a pair of Binos (Binoculars) for traces of the enemy.

It's just continuous instruction and training, but that's why I joined.

The CO said the tour was a dam good effort and good skills!

On another tour of Norway we had been instructed by a switched on Royal Marine called Steve who was a mate of one of my colleagues at St D's although obviously I didn't know him at this point. This Royal Marine took our section on a patrol in Norway.

He won the Military Medal down in the Falklands War and is very courageous.

All of the lads got some valuable reconnaissance and patrolling experience and then we came out of the field and boarded HMS *Fearless*.

Next winter deployment we teamed up with the Brigade and were taking part in Ex Cold Winter. A tremendous number of Sea King choppers were ferrying the Royal Marines to separate locations. We would huddle together in our sticks 'groups' and the Cpl would guide the Chopper in to collect the Royal Marines who were congregated in a stick. This meant they were basically huddled together and low on the ground to make themselves as hard a target as possible. That tour of Norway was well attended and all the Royal Marines got a successful amount of experience in working with choppers and in defensive positions.

I spoke to Bill Wright at the Unit and apparently he had previously been running the Mountain Leader Section at Commando Training Centre. This is what Bill said:

I have been based up here for about one and a half years. This is the nearest posting I have been to my family. I have been in the Royal Marines 20 years now and I have served in every unit. My favourite Unit has got to be 45 Cdo and that is because of the comradeship around and in Arbroath the Jocks are very special and the Unit is quite adaptable. I feel drawn to 45 Cdo; Well I like to think we are all extremely experienced.

I was at Stonehouse Barracks and became part of the Mountain Leader Cadre and they are quite special, Actually one Cpl from this Unit is with them now.

My role at this unit is to train all of A Company that is all the Commando Trained Ranks, basically anyone with a Green Beret. To keep them current with their training and run the Winter Deployment to Norway. To practise with their Field Firing, Survival skills, Soldering skills and of course Mountain Training. Of course all Royal Marines are expected to be super fit, well it's essential and necessary to enable the Royal Marines to support 3 Cdo Bde.

I did join when the Falklands Islands kicked off and from then to now the difference is immense. You do not have to train wearing your boots but whilst taking part in the Commando Tests your boots must be worn. You still have to maintain exactly the same high standards. You do complete the same training, regardless of which unit you are with including the RMR. It certainly is the same once you achieve your Green Beret and have been to Norway or America several times and when you have served with the Corps. Certainly now the recruits are eased into training. The people who are joining are used to trainers and computers. It is so different from the type of recruits that were joining 20 years ago. Now the recruits come from a much softer environment. Previously good blokes have failed and that is because of injuries; it certainly is pathetic. That a man can get to week 19 and then sustain an injury and that would be his career over! Currently the Royal Marines find it very difficult to recruit and they have sent exceptional men away but the men that pass the Commando Course are still experts.

The RMR might be similar to the Para's or 23 SAS (Special Air Service) because they receive the same Special Training as our lads. My thoughts on the TA are that it's more of a social set-up, but that's only my opinion. I feel the Royal Marine Reserve (RMR) is definitely just as committed as their Regular Counterparts. Well not many people have heard of the RMR but it's not the TA. The majority of society, including most of the ex -servicemen think that the RMR is the TA, which it is not. Actually it has nothing to do with the Army. It is actually part of the Royal Navy but only a minute part. The RMR'S most primary roles are amphibious forces and supporting 3 Commando Brigade.

Another trip down South and apparently Prince Edward was visiting and afterwards there was to be an activity weekend, to which all St Dunstaners were invited to attend. I was present in the gym when his Royal Highness toured the building. Quite a number of displays were in progress, personal craft and picture framing were on display. Then his Royal Highness Prince Edward visited the gym. Grant had me flexing my muscles and I was demonstrating how some of the equipment worked. Grant explained how some of the Royal Marines had raised the money for all of the air pressure apparatus. Then he was gone with the wave of a crop!

That signalled to Grant that the activities would commence. Every man and his dog was present. We first went abseiling and a guy called Dave assisted me onto the cliffs. Presently he owns a bike shop in Brighton. He is all alone in Brighton, so go along and visit and buy a bike from him!

It was very memorable because I ripped the backside clean out of my designer tracksuit leggings,and therefore I was gutted. I was showing off, as you do. I remembered how to do it but I think I should have had the extra support because I rolled and ended up going down with my head facing down. Of course I had been an expert before the injury.

Dave assisted on the trek from the transport to the steady incline leading to the cliffs. The next activity was canoeing but they were two-men canoes and you couldn't easily go fast as the result would be to kill yourself or someone else, not that you wanted to. They were too stable and I asked Grant to let us go in some one-man canoes, to which he declined. He just muttered 'Safety First.'

Then we went on some tandems and we ended up

riding to the White Horse, which is a venue for the majority of St Dunstaners. We had been blessed with some fine weather, I said to Dave 'At least it hasn't rained yet! It normally does in the UK.'

Everybody piled into the bar and there were quite a number of members of the Army present, primarily to assist and give their support. As I've already stated alcohol is used as a recreation period. We were then onto 'It's a Knockout'. Grant had put a lot of time and effort into the weekend and I certainly appreciated it, even if nobody else did.

Ovingdean, for anybody who doesn't know Brighton, is all on a hill, so therefore the House is on a hill. Grant had a large container about halfway down and a large pulley attached to a sort of hand-cranked pulley that was then relayed to another container. The idea of the game was to attach a bucket full of water to the pulley and send the bucket on its way to be collected in the top container. The water was then measured and the winning team were informed to get the beers in. As a result, it's your round!

It was time for another bike race, and I again trained intensively, determined this time to achieve an extremely fast time. The previous time we had completed the race on a child's bike. Over the phone, Grant and I discussed about purchasing a new bike, which St D's would pay for using the funds that I had raised on my first bike ride.

I flew down South and Grant and I went up to where the shop was situated and had a trial run. We both liked what we saw and tested. We then returned to the House and told everyone we saw about the marvellous and very fast trike we had been viewing. I then returned home to attend training at a later date.

Grant Cooper with Steve on the second Bike Ride
with the new trike

I had never really stopped training since the previous
bike ride the year before but this time I was determined
to achieve a fantastic time. Well I was always determined,
but I was extra prepared. I attended St Dunstans
approximately twice just to get some experience in on
the bike, but unfortunately the bike was not there. I was
gutted, but there was nothing that could be done.
However, under the circumstances and considering I had
come a long way, training commenced in the gym. Grant
said, 'You need some leg work,' To which I totally
disagreed as my legs were cut to ribbons, though my
quads, hamstrings and my calves were certainly well
developed. I suppose it did fill in the week and I was
able to go out with various friends in and around Brighton.

I returned to St Dunstans for the last time prior to the
bike ride. The trike was present and it was causing quite
a stir among the staff of St D's. Grant and myself took

the trike out and bumped in to another St Dunstaner. It was Steve Sparks, a former Royal Marine, who was also going to take part in the London to Brighton Bike Ride.

The water was calm as it lapped at the supports of the Palace Pier. Brighton was certainly a hectic city even early in the morning. The sun was just beginning to show its smiling face and the hustle and bustle of city streets became apparent. We had a whet (drink) and then parted company; we would see Steve again for the bike ride.

Grant informed me an Iron Man Competition was going on and some members of staff including Janis and Gay from the computer department had come along to lend their support. Grant and I tagged along just for valuable experience on the road. Then Mike and I from the gym took the trike out for a long way along the coast. Grant and I did quite a number of very steep inclines and then the training was completed. I was well and truly exhausted and I needed a rest period. Consequently I did return home for a rest and recuperation period before returning down South for the fabulous 'Race'.

The weather was cloudy and I breathed a sigh of relief to myself. I muttered to nobody in particular 'Last year, it was like riding through a furnace.'

Grant got all the various bikes out. It was incredibly early and I was hurrying around the building singing songs about Sunderland Football club. This time there wasn't any one present from the Corps, only ex Royal Marines, Sparky and me. We all loaded onto the transport and headed up to London. We had thought we would miss the majority of cyclists but sadly not. We had managed to manoeuvre our vehicle through the traffic to arrive in time to get equipped for the race.

We were all edging a selection of totally different machines forward. We lined up and then we were off.

The going was tough and nobody from the St D's team came whizzing past us because of the speed we raised.

Mike and Dave from the Gym were acting as Grant's backup and they had cycled away to rendezvous with Grant and myself. Dave Goldsmith then swapped places with Grant and we carried on. Gary Lomas and Linda Stringer came rushing past.

Grant and Mike dislodged the chain on their tandem and were in need of some support. Ian Hepborn managed to repair a certain number of the St D's Team's cycles and we would have been lost without that talented man. Grant said 'Luckily for us, he's not just a wizard with mobility training.' We then all teamed up at a water stop.

Dave is concerned that Mike is absent when he needs him. We head off and it is apparent that the trike is experiencing difficulties. The lower cog has become mangled in the chain and is totally and completely unfixable, according to Ian the specialist. The team stay with me and Dave to assist on the many inclines. Billy, who is Ian's partner, and Gary help, along with Linda Stringer. Grant and Mike arrive and they have got to make a decision. Sadly, my bike ride is OVER!

CHAPTER 7

It's All Greek to Me

After the severity of nearly being killed, I needed a holiday. Somewhere hot was the suggestion made by me to Lance the ex-policeman who said that he would come along for a beer or two. We got booked up and flew out of London Gatwick. I was still at St D's so we asked Col Bray and the Training Wing if I could slip away for a week. It was sanctioned and we boarded a jet and headed for Rhodes.

Well I had been to Greece once previously but that was 7 years ago. I knew the people were extremely friendly and what is more that the food was delicious. Lance and I, both tired, booked into a hotel. At this stage, two sticks still accompanied me! The year was 1993 and it was two years after the tragic encounter with a truck.

We went into the old town and looked at the old German ruins from the World War II and shivered at the thought of what it must have been like living in an occupied country. Your worst nightmare only much worse.

The sea was extremely choppy and the wind was making it sound like a hurricane was about to be unleashed upon us. Unfortunately the rocks were causing a fair problem so consequently we stayed around the pool, where there was this 'bird' with the most fabulous and gigantic tits that I have ever seen. I said to Lance 'You can expect massive melons on a big lady but she was extremely fit and as a result, essence.' Lance just said 'I've seen it all before!' I said to Lance 'So have I, but she was very attractive and certainly quite fit for all she had a child.' Lance just laughed and said 'How do you know, with your eyesight problems?' So we did spend a lot of our free time around the swimming pool!

Lance hired a vehicle and both of us toured the island, as there were many sites to see. There was a small piece of Greek history, a statue of Colossus standing over the harbour. Unfortunately it collapsed in 226 BC and is currently replaced by a deer. We visited quite a number of tavernas and restaurants. This particular one played live Greek music and Locals used to come from the four corners of the island to attend the show and experience the atmosphere. Well, we used to go there every night after our meal and it was certainly lively.

It was only a short way from the hotel so I used to walk with my two sticks. It was quite beneficial. I tried my luck at Greek dancing and ironically I became a 'Pretty Good Mover' with the Greeks supporting me. It was fantastic. We were eating one night and I heard an Englishman order his meal in Greek. I was gob-smacked and totally impressed! That was it; I made a vow to learn Greek as soon as I returned home to the Northeast, even with my eyesight difficulties. I was busy learning how to play chess so off I went hunting for a really good chess set. There were many variations to choose from. Unfortunately they were all Greek Gods and in so much fine detail that I couldn't make the pieces out but I purchased an onyx set, just as an ornament and in case my eyes improved. Chess is an incredible game and you have to be quite intelligent to actually compete in tournaments. I do confess to being just an average player so I don't do competitions. Well I only play now and then but I have a large English set, which is very big and the pieces are quite clear. Unfortunately I can't make out the pieces on the Greek set.

Greece is certainly a great country and the weather is fantastic and as a result we both had an incredible holiday. The weather makes quite a difference to the country you live in. I love this country, without the rain, but still I like Greece very much. Returning to the UK took a long time and was tiresome. The thing about Greece I don't like is the sanitation facilities. It is so primitive putting your toilet paper in a bin, so disgusting and the poor maid is required to empty it.

A St D's driver collected us and that was my recreation time complete.

Home visiting the gym and going swimming becomes a touch tedious after a while but I love training. It is essential to keep the body fit and to keep the mind active. Subsequently I attended college to study the Greek language as I'd always said I would and whatever I say, I do.

As far back as when I was on my holidays with Lindsey's mam I can still remember showing an interest and stating 'Wouldn't it be brilliant to be able to speak the language?'

I did learn how to speak Spanish with Richard, this was after I could speak Greek exceptionally.

When I first came back up to the Northeast I used an agency and the manager, who was also the owner of the company, used to drive me to and from the college where I was studying Greek language. The teacher was Greek and I got on quite well with her, so much so I asked her to give me private lessons in the Greek way of communicating, to which she happily agreed. No wonder I was her top student. I used to practise constantly, every spare minute God sent. Inea used to photocopy the lesson into large print and I used to study for a long period at home. Her daughter was gorgeous so naturally I took her out to the Dun Cow at Burnmoor just for a touch of English cuisine but sadly it didn't measure up to the Greeks' delicious and irresistible menus. She had a Greek name that reminded me of the Greek word for Wednesday, which is Tetarti.

Then I attended Redcar Road College in Sunderland. My knowledge of Greek progressed to a satisfactory standard and I decided to attend college again. I went and sat next to Anne and Den Jenkinson and Anne's best friend Jan Towns. They used to assist by copying down the words that were written on the blackboard in large print because I didn't have sufficient vision, although by this stage I could speak Greek very well. The teachers were definitely impressed with my efforts in spite of the fact that I had been injured. They thought it was incredible and it just shows what can be achieved if you put your mind to it.

After I left college I still wanted to learn even more so once again I enrolled back at college. Jane, the teacher, was married to a Greek and quite frequently she would take a lesson at the College near to where I lived and I would visit to be taught. I had to pass quite a lot of tests and I did receive two certificates after a long and tiring course. Jane was great with me and I think a teacher knows if you want to succeed and will help such a student in her own time.

It was Jane who plunged me into the finals of the Adult Achievers Awards and my Mam was present. The year was 1997 and I did study at Sunderland College. This was approximately 5½ years after the anonymous 4-ton truck had smacked me.

Again, I received some special assistance at the college with Jane handing out her expertise. I was well chuffed because Greek is one of the hardest languages to learn and especially after a life-threatening escapade, which had so affected my eyesight. They have a completely unique alphabet. The Greek alphabet has 24 letters unlike the English one, which has 26 letters and are quite easily recognized. Plus it made matters worse with my eyesight, but if I had been totally blind – well it doesn't bear thinking about! I do feel sorry for the lads who are totally blind, especially Clive.

Clive gets on with his life pretty well and he is a member of the St D's Archery Team. As Gary Lomas said 'It's about ability and not disability.' I agree with Gary and stated that if you put your mind to achieve a certain task, you will succeed. The whole of St Dunstans is remarkable and totally amazing, not to mention the men there.

Kevin Weatherley was acting as my driver in 1999 – 2000. He is an ex-policeman and is married to Jan, who I met at college. Naturally he is a big guy.

Anne and Den emigrated to Melbourne in Australia. I used to attend college with them and also with Kev's wife Jan. Kev assisted me to book up. I assume it was only because it was the other side of the world and because he and Jan had just returned from visiting Anne and Den. Well I wasn't going to say 'You just stay in the car, mate!'

Kev visited HMS *Illustrious* with me. This ship was used in the Falklands War. I had met a Field Gunner called Richard and he used to assist with the St Dunstaners. Consequently he did actually invite us onboard for a look around. I received quite a bit of alcohol and rolled up the stairs heading for the upper decks. A sober Kev and I left. Most of the crew were on leave and unfortunately we didn't meet many matlows. Just for the smart arses in the world you have to go down the stairs to the mess as it is in the middle of the ship.

In the year of 2001 I visited Australia for a bit of a holiday and to visit my friends that I had met at college; they lived on a farm.

I spoke to Chipper Stilton about going and he told me he had a brother in Perth, which was in Western Australia and that if he could get time away from diving, we could kill two birds with one stone.

On one of my training visits down to St D's I met an older man from World War II and we got pissed. We got talking and I informed him of my forthcoming trip to Australia and ironically he told me he had a daughter who lived in Perth but what was more of a coincidence was that he was a former Royal Marine.

Apparently he took part in the attack on the Iron Coast to rid the world of a dictator.

He was called Jack and we became close friends. He must have had a terrible time; he was so reluctant to speak about it. Some men will, some men will not, but it is their prerogative. Jack said 'I'll come and see you when you participate in the Bike Ride and I'll sponsor you.' I said 'Okay I'll visit your daughter when I go to Australia.'

It was early September 2001 when I flew out of Newcastle to rendervous with Chip. We flew out of London and refuelled at Singapore to arrive in Melbourne, Australia approximately 20 hours later. With the time difference it does seem much longer. The most obvious thing was just how dead clean and new the place was. I said to Chip 'Puts the UK to shame'. We were met by Den and drove to a cottage where we would stay for the duration of our holiday. Den loaned us an estate car. Soon we got accustomed to the local beer 'VB' – Victoria Bitter. Anne and Den took us to a bird sanctuary, and to see lots of animals, and many other sights.

Chip and I went off on our own into the city and I ate crocodile and Skippy (Kangaroo). I will not speak about what took place next. We returned via the local railways and returned to our cottage.

I was busy sleeping, Then I heard Chip scream 'Steve! Steve!' I got out of bed and rushed the best I could to the TV room. What I saw was terrible! We saw pictures of planes flying directly into the World Trade Centre. The number of casualties was immense and we were totally stunned. We thought of all the innocent members of society that were involved in this insane event. Having to board a plane to head straight to Perth we were definitely concerned. At a later date we would need to face that long haul when returning to the UK.

That makes me remember what took place shortly after I returned home. One day I was my usual chirpy and very vocal self and I boarded the British Airways Flight bound for London Gatwick. In the wake of September the 11th, I stood up, not thinking and stated, and I quote! 'I am a Marine and if there are any Arabs on board I will kill them.' I thought that was a totally harmless remark, but to other members of society, sadly not! I thought I would reassure passengers who were afraid to fly but unfortunately, a security guard appeared and informed me to exit the flight. At no point did I try to resist. I am fully responsible for my actions but couldn't they see what my intentions had been or the funny side of the incident? I do understand that the airlines are a touch sensitive at present but it was only a joke. Needless to say I boarded the plane at a later time. Incredibly the very next flight!

So you see I was completely innocent and anybody with half a brain should have realized that I was no threat to the aircraft and certainly not to any of the passengers.

Both of us arrived at Perth to be met and accompanied by Jack's daughter the great Cindy and Chip's brother, Alan. I booked into a very interesting motel that was next to the River Swaney. Cindy had some holidays so she and Alan showed us the sights. How surprising it should be a brewery first and then a beautiful chocolate factory afterwards. We visited a number of restaurants and bars and Alan took us all over Western Australia.

The great Cindy took me down the beach and ironically we were practically the only ones on there. Of course I knew that there was no Ozone layer, but it was only once. The great Cindy and I went out constantly. On one such occasion, Cindy, Chip, Alan and I went up to a lady friend's of Alan, who had three lovely children. We had a fantastic meal and that was cool! I did say I would return one day.

I was a touch anxious boarding a plane home for a long haul flight after that insane event but security is regarded as an essential part of flying these days.

CHAPTER 8

Personal Accounts

On one occasion I was visiting St D's, this time for training purposes. The first place I visited was the lounge and I saw Adrian from the bar and was talking to him and then a familiar figure comes round the corner and it is Ian Millard. Ian was in the Royal Air Force and he had been in training with me the second time I was at St D's, after I had returned from Ticehurst. Ian informed me he had been in the RAF for a total of 14 years and that's a considerable lengthy spell. He told me he had served in such countries as Denmark, Germany, Gibraltar, Cyprus and The Falkland Islands. Ian had been a driver and he even learnt how to drive a crane. His duties made him available to drive any vehicle, so naturally he passed his HGV test with the highest ability.

Sadly he lost his eyesight because of a medical condition and was admitted into St D's.

Now he takes part in a tremendous number of running events. He has participated in the Iron Man, London Marathon and many other events and raised a substantial amount of money for various charities along the routes.

I also had a quick chat with Dave Powell. Dave is a very experienced soldier. Ironically he was at the exact same camp as me in Norway. Dave has served in Northern Ireland and Norway on a handful of occasions.

I had some spare time so I interviewed Nigel Whitely regarding his Service career and how he lost his eyesight.

I joined the Royal Navy at the Age of 15 at HMS St Vincent at Gosport in Hampshire and that was a long time ago in July 1960, nine years before you were hatched, Steve.

My basic training consisted of basic electrics, Naval customs, climbing over the mast, which was 124 feet high, cross country running, rugby and all aspects of sport and that took place over a very long and sometimes quite tiresome year.

I left St Vincent the following year, 1961, and I went to HMS Collingwood, which is in Fareham, and trained as a electrician After being in the Royal Navy eight years I was in patrolling submarines but I then transferred to the Medical Branch all duties and from there I was given a place on an All Arms Commando course, which I passed admirably.

That then qualified me to work with Med squadron, Commando Logs attached to the glorious 3 Cdo Bde, then I went to the Fleet Air Arm Field Gun Crew and I was a medic with the Field Gun crew in 1969 and 1972. Little did I know that in the future I would become a St Dunstaner myself. I also served in a various array of hospitals. I quickly became involved with St D's and I became a Dog 'escort'.

I was shore based in Mauritius in the Indian Ocean. Also I served in Kenya, Singapore, and Simons town in South Africa. Whilst on ships we visited all round the Indian Ocean, Japan, South America, Australia and the United States of America. When I was attached to the Royal Marines I was in Northern Ireland and Lebanon. I did serve down the Falkland Islands when the campaign was in progress. I was with a sea mine clearance unit and there was a phenomenal amount of mines. We went in before the bulk of our main Task Force had arrived and I was on the RMS the Royal Battleship St Eleanor. We were actually the Mother Ship, which was a Civilian Ship for the SAS and the famous SBS that don't receive the credit they deserve. They did the incurtions against Argentina along with the SAS. A Royal Marine Cpl also lost his life with 22 SAS as an Albatross flew into the rotor blades of the chopper they were travelling in and crashed. A lot of men lost their lives during that war for Queen and Country.

The main reason my sight has deteriorated is that when I was serving with the 846 Naval Air Commando squadron in Lebanon Units of 41 and 42 were acting as back up. Unfortunately I caught an infection in my eyes and in my heart and also my circulation became a major problem and because of that, my sight became considerably worse and I actually lost the sight in one eye in 1987. As a result, sadly I was discharged from the Royal Navy. Most of the sight in my other eye went on Millennium Eve in 1999.

The year 2000 did not bring back my sight and I became a St Dunstaner on 3 February 2000.

After the interview with Nigel, I then spoke to Billy Baxter. Billy is absolutely brilliant and he has a wicked sense of humour.

I joined the Army as a Junior Leader at the young age of 15 and a half years, in the Royal Artillery at Nuneaton barracks, and I did join in January 1980. After completing my training at the Junior Leader's regiment Royal Artillery I went to the King's Troop Royal horse Artillery where I did a Mounted Gunner's course for a total of six months.

After completing the course I transferred to 1 RHA on the equipment FH70, which was based in North Yorkshire. Then I went to Germany and this was just before the Falklands Campaign. During the Falklands War our Regiment, E Battery, did an 8 month operational tour in Northern Ireland. I served in Bosnia for 8 months during Operation Resolute 2.

Throughout the Forces, especially in a fighting Trp, every soldier wants to experience combat, basically out of curiosity and to put their training into effect. There our mission was basically controlling the ceasefire and controlling all avenues of war in factions between the Croats, Muslim and the Serb Forces. Operation Resolute 1 was part of the United Nations force responsible for enforcing a no-fly zone over Bosnia. NATO then took over enforcing the no-fly zone. Our role out there was to provide a show of force, by forceful means if necessary, and control the war between factions, protecting the civilian population, men, women and children, against acts of war and the militia.

Our main role was peace keeping and we were allowed to implement rules by using force, e. g. if we saw an act of war, Serb forces shooting at unarmed civilians we were tasked to return fire.

Where we were in Bosnia there were a lot of mass graves where whole villages had been wiped out. We were tasked to lift the bodies out and place them on stretchers. It was a disgusting job. Then I was tasked to shoot wild dogs that were running away with bits of human remains. Whilst taking part in this process I did receive a horrible eye infection in both of my optic nerves.

When this occurred I was totally devastated and

my life was in a shambles and I was pissed off and most definitely suicidal. I'm married with three beautiful children and at that time I did think it was the end of my life. Carol, my wife spotted an article for St D's in a magazine the Army had passed on and they contacted me immediately.

I arrived at St D's in June 2000 and not knowing what to expect I stood to attention, even the cleaners I was calling Sir and Mam. Well I didn't know what to say or to expect.

My life has progressed to a satisfactory standard and at present I'm giving some speeches for St D's and in the process gaining a lot of experience with public speaking. I am also involved with a motorcycle display team that's with the Royal Artillery called the Flying Gunners. They are assisting me to attempt to break the land speed blind solo record, and that takes place in August 2003. I will be trying to ride a high-powered Motorcycle solo at over 150-mph with the aid of an intercom and flanked by two outriders. I participate in various displays and I am the opening ride and when the person explains I am totally blind and the reaction is a one of amazement and a hell of a lot of admiration. As far as I know I am the only totally blind person in a Motorcycle Display team in the world.

In the Army I drove motorcycles and I was also an instructor. Well, I feel my life is full again. It's grown on me, my disability, although I didn't receive any further injuries. But I have had immense injuries involving my bike. I did take my kneecap off and had a dislocated shoulder and many other injuries including breaking every bone in my hand. You know Steve; it's less frightening doing a pyramid in a display *team than actually crossing a road using my white cane. It frightens me more just walking down the street, and this is the message I want to get across to society. I want to make people aware of blindness, also I want to make people aware of all conflicts, and needless to say, St Dunstans.*

Billy still drives on; defeating all obstacles set before him. Since giving this interview Billy has successfully accomplished the Land Speed Record on Two Wheels for a blind person, reaching a speed of 164–9 mph, which is a vast achievement. He is an amazing character, as most are in HM Forces. There are some wild men but they are totally committed to the cause and very experienced and certainly a laugh.

Going down to the Cenotaph for the Remembrance Parade was an annual event. When November comes upon us, it is a time to remember those of your immediate family and friends who have fallen in past conflicts.

Jeff and I would be collected by a St D's driver at London and driven to the hotel, where we would stay, courtesy of St D's. It was as if God himself was coming to inspect the whole procedure. There was certainly a tremendous amount of preparation and planning went into the whole event. I saw quite a lot of old friends. We all got pissed as per usual but not in the bar as it was just too expensive, so we did search for an alternative watering hole.

The next morning you are up at the crack of dawn as the queues are immense, still you have to eat. Then you are told to meet your guides and board the transport for Horse Guards to alight the transport and sit shivering for at least an hour. My guides have been no other than Major General Keils, Col Courtney, Col Babbington,

Colour Sgt K Armstrong, Sgt Dennis, Sgt Patterson, Mne Lee and this year's parade will be Mne Rundle.

You see you have to meet your escorts quite early, but I always travel down South with one of the lads from our Unit. Most have either been promoted, left the Unit or like Jeff, have been medically discharged because of his leg. Jeff was also a PTI at our unit, when he took the recruits for physical they received a serious beasting. Also Jeff is an HGV driver and of course his is AWT (Artic Warfare Trained) and he did achieve this in Arctic Norway.

The year 2002 was a time for remembering. Jeff Rundle and I flew down to London for the Parade but sadly I missed it because of illness. From the minute I arrived I was confined to my hotel room, so Jeff got pissed independently. I must have picked up the illness on the plane. Well that's the only suggestion that is feasible because as you know the air on a plane doesn't circulate very well.

I rose on the Sunday. All the St Dunstaners were on the Parade and when they returned all would enjoy a commemoration lunch with a number of speeches.

Jeff and I enjoyed our meal in a separate room, just in case I was horribly sick all over everyone else's meal. I spoke to a fair few St Dunstaners; and made some phone calls to enable me to find out some useful information.

A former Royal Marine who has gone through a totally terrible time is Tony Haskey. I managed to speak to Tony after the Cenotaph.

I joined the Royal Marines on 9 September 1975 and it was agonizingly tough.

I travelled down to Deal for my first 13 weeks. I met up with some lads who were all good eggs. We were all nervous as hell and only 16, we hadn't even begun to bloody shave yet. The lads I met then I still keep in touch with to this day. We were all looking forward to the intense and extremely difficult training and a lifelong commitment to the Realm.

When we arrived at Deal we were formed into 214 Trp and the Trp started with 109 young men. We were then beasted constantly and quite a lot of men dropped out, actually after 13 weeks we were down to 54 young recruits. We then moved up to Lympstone and were expected to take another 30 weeks of intensive Commando Training.

On completion of this a very proud Tony Haskey emerged as a fully-fledged Royal Marine Commando. My first posting was to join 41 Cdo, unfortunately this unit has now been disbanded, but once there we did take part in the Royal Tournament of 1976.

As a GD (General Duties) Marine I was to become part of E Company along with several of my oppos that I joined up with. During my time at 41 Cdo I did take part in Jungle Training in Brunei that lasted for a total of 8 weeks. We then were allowed a run ashore where we all got completely wrecked. I also took part in an UN exercise in Turkey with the US Marines.

I was caught having sex in the Officers' Galley and therefore got banged up for 28 days.

Six months before the end of my time in Malta 7 Royal Marines were asked to stay behind to form a special Company called Salerno Company. The aim of this Company was to guard the airfield and camp for the RAF.

In 1980 I was posted to 42 Cdo at Bickly Barracks and during my posting I did two tours of Northern

Ireland. During my two Tours of Northern Ireland we were involved in several incidents that helped to make the Tours very memorable.

I was also lucky enough to spend six months with 42 Cdo in Hong Kong working with the Hong Kong police on Border control. Our task there was to stop and detain illegal immigrants coming in from China. Once the illegal immigrants were caught we would hand them over to the Hong Kong police. Whilst taking part in this task we were billeted in a camp called Fanling camp in the new territories. We also had some time in the city so this proved to be an excellent run ashore.

In 1982/83 I was then posted back to Deal and roomer control informed us that the Corps was asking for volunteers that would form 12 Trp and would work out of South Amagh.

I volunteered for this with all my Oppos and a lot of them had served there previously.

Disastrously one of my close Oppos was killed in a large bomb blast whilst out on patrol with two members of 2 Para and two Royal Marines and sadly this was only two months before our tour ended.

Towards the end of the tour I noticed my night vision was poor and it was becoming extremely difficult to see at night. I came to the conclusion my eyes had just deteriorated because of everything I had done in the Royal Marines and I thought every Royal Marine was the same.

I was then asked to select a specialist qualification and I decided I would like to become a driver. I went down to Bestbrook camp for a thorough medical examination. During this examination I was asked if I had any problems, so I told them about my eyes *even though I had mentioned it several times previously whilst serving with 42 Cdo. When I was examined a doctor looked into my eyes and then sent me to a specialist eye institute. Once there I was given eye examination after examination and at the end of the second day, I was told I had an incurable eye condition that would result in me becoming totally blind. As you could imagine I was a touch pissed off but then I was informed the condition could move slow or fast but it was a hell of a lot better than being dead.*

Because of my eye condition I was offered a clerk's course at the Commando Training Centre. No man joins the Royal Marines to become a clerk but I had no choice because the Royal Marines could not allow me to continue in my current capacity as a GD Marine.

It was a way of staying in the Royal Marines, so I took the course six months after returning from Northern Ireland. After completion of the course I was posted to RM Poole, as a pay clerk. Unfortunately this only lasted four months.

Then I was offered the post of pay clerk with 3 Raiding Squadron in Hong Kong for 30 months and this was a married person's draft so I had my wife and son with me. During my time in 3 RSRM I took part in a tremendous amount of sports. Our job in Hong Kong was to patrol the waterways with fast pursuit craft around the various islands which border Hong Kong.

When I returned from overseas I went straight back to Poole as a clerk. Whilst there I completed a Junior Command course but due to my poor vision I failed the course.

After 11 years dedicated service, tragically I was asked to leave the Royal Marines on Medical grounds. Well the Royal Marine Commandos was my life.

After spending several years trying to come to terms with my deteriorating eye condition I was appointed a social worker. It was through another ex serviceman (Percy Pongo) that I found out about St Dunstans. Pongo explained about St D's and the work they do for all ex servicemen and that they could assist me with a variety of aspects of my life. I was invited to Ovingdean at Brighton where I received a fantastic amount of beneficial information and mobility training. I stayed for quite a considerable lengthy spell.

From there I went on a one year course at the Royal National Institute for the Blind (RNIB) and because it was residential I took full advantage of this. I managed to pass a computer course and also my GCSE in English, Maths and RSA Typing. I was delighted to pass my very difficult course at Hereford. In a different degree it reminded me of my training but only in the classroom, nothing resembled the extreme punishment that I had been inflicting on myself.

After leaving Hereford I went on a two year business course at Bournemouth University.

The course was tough, but nothing more than I had come into contact with previously.

With the assistance of my family and friends I managed to pass with flying colours.

I was lucky enough to gain full time employment as an assistant analyst working for a company called Ken 25 software. I have now progressed to the Manager's position and it is a worthwhile career. As you may know Computers are an object of the future.

In June 2002 I was sadly diagnosed with having the big C (Cancer). I had the illness in the Tongue, Tonsils and face and after a 14-hour operation I was sent to an intensive care Unit. In three days I was actually sitting up in hospital looking like Desperate Dan out of a cartoon and I spoke like Mr Bean. Since then I have had to learn to swallow, eat and talk properly. A plate was fitted inside my mouth to enable me to speak clearly and this did shorten the distance between my tongue and the roof of my mouth.

Whilst under going training at St D's I met a wonderful lady and so incredibly caring, we plan to marry. Having worked as a catering manageress for some time she is an expert cook and that's not all she is an expert at!

Her name is the attractive Cosy and she is remarkable and one hell of a catch. Good effort Tony, you deserve her!

As General Keils said, 'It takes a lot to hold a good man down'. He is an amazing and courageous man and it must be because he did serve in the Royal Marines. You know what they say: Once a Marine, always a Marine and it's certainly true!

So the Corps lives on!

Sgt Armstrong is a former member of the Army. He then joined the Royal Marines Reserve. One year, he stated he would escort me to the Cenotaph Parade. He was the Head PTI (Physical Training Instructor). When I first joined I found it difficult to climb the 30fFt ropes with full kit and a weapon but Keith had a procedure. Knees up, lay back, short, long hand on top. We did a tremendous amount of shuttle runs and roaring 20s and of course circuits. Of course we were Mega Fit. We would run as a Trp (Troop) to the Tits (these were hills shaped like 2 tits) and then a beasting would commence. Down 10 star jumps up and make a big circle and keep running round. Down 10 squat thrusts and upkeep running round; down 10 bastards and up, keep running round; down 10 press-ups and up and keep running round. Down 10 sit ups and up, keep running round. All Stop! Down 10 Burpees and up 5 minutes sprinting on the spot, holding your arms stretched out, hands facing down and bringing your legs up to slap your quads off your hands. Fall in on road below. Running back to the Unit. You would hear the Command, touch the ground with your right hand and continue running, with your left hand and continue running. Jump in the air and head an imaginary ball. Jeff shouts, 'last man to the yard gets the beers in.' Fortunately I wasn't last so we all raced to the yard.

At the yard the Sgt screams 'Two ranks in front of me, go. Fireman's carrys, commence'. You had to pick a man, equal size and weight and then run the length of a football pitch in 90 seconds. Of course you had kit and a weapon at the Commando Training Centre.

After that you had to demonstrate how a regain was completed – crawl over a rope hanging from two buildings then hang underneath the rope and get back on the rope under your own steam and continue crawling over the rope. Then a few shuttle runs.

That was the training complete for that night and as you could imagine it pissed down.

At this stage we had completed a phase 1 course at CTC RM (Commando Training Centre Royal Marines) and when we attended a Commando Course at CTC Royal Marines we would be ready. Of course until you pass your Commando Course and earn your green beret, the training standards certainly become even more intense, if it could get any harder, but now it is expected of you. The training takes at the very least a year.

I caught up with Tom Roddy and asked him about his Service Career in the RAF.

I did join up in 1958 and that proves how old I am, Steve! I enlisted for National Service with the RAF. I did sign up for three extra years with the RAF rather than the Army. It wasn't for me, all that rolling among the mud and foliage. Having spent three years in Germany I returned to the North East. Due to unemployment at home I decided to sign up for another nine years. Life progressed until I found myself signing up again for another 10 years, hence serving my full 22 years.

Initially I was trained as an Operations Clerk but during my Service Career it was renamed to Assistant Air Traffic Controller.

My basic training was about 12 weeks and then we proceeded to RAF Shorebridge for seven weeks and then to Germany. I have also served in Borneo and Libya. It was the year of 1993 and I was demobbed from the RAF when my eyesight deteriorated and I was in and out of hospital.

Eventually I was asked to visit London for an eye test and as a result found myself going to St Dunstan's at Ovingdean near to Brighton in '94 for about three months. I was actually made a St Dunstaner in 1995, one year after been admitted for training.

The training I received helped a great deal. A very skilful teacher who went by the name of Terry Walker taught me Braille. Learning to use a computer was extremely tough but with the excellent tuition displayed by Janis Sharp, I was successful. Well I was taught a tremendous amount of very useful and beneficial information.

Whilst training myself I met this Russian from St Petersburg and we became close friends so much so I have visited Russia twice. His name was Nikolai and we still keep in touch to this day.

Having been in the Forces I am a keen sportsman and used to participate in Master Swimming even when I had left the RAF, but sadly that had to cease when my condition got much worse. I met you in the swimming pool because I still like to keep my body supple and all the joints moving freely.

At present I live with Jenny, my partner, in Darlington. Jenny takes part in the Great North Run quite frequently and we both enjoy an array of sports.

I asked Tony Watson to come around so that I could pick his brain and find out some useful information. Tony spoke to me with reference to his Royal Navy Career:

I joined the Royal Navy on 24 January 1978 at the young age of 16 years.

My initial training took place at HMS Raleigh. To the best of my knowledge it lasted six or seven weeks and that was all fitness and drill. Then I went to HMS Collingwood to receive a further ten weeks training and my Specialist training which was my Electrical Training. This took place at the Electrical School. Once I had passed out I joined HMS Coventry as an Ordnance electrical Mechanic.

In 1986 I went to Northern Ireland. Once out in Northern Ireland I joined HMS Cygnet. This small ship was the last ship in the Royal Navy with an open bridge. It was a Third Class Ship, a cygnet. This ship was the smallest in the Navy. You know

Steve, to give people an idea of just what I am talking about, just watch an Old World War II film. You will see the officers searching the ocean for the enemy, standing on the bridge.

We were backwards and forwards to Rosyth, and to prove how small we were, the ship could actually fit through the Caledonian Canal, which runs the width of Scotland. This is a sort of river with a number of locks and it goes directly all the way from the West to the East Coast so you can imagine just how small we were.

In Northern Ireland we used to patrol in and around Belfast Harbour and we had a small contingent of Royal Marines with a sniffer dog. We used to search all the cargo ships for ammunition, explosives and of course weapons. The terrorists were extremely successful and you were never going to find any because they had whole rooms welded behind other rooms so it was impossible to detect them. 99% of people coming into Northern Ireland were completely innocent and you were just there as a deterrent. On the way into Belfast Harbour and actually leaving I was on the GPMG (General Purpose Machine Gun) covering all flanks – this was situated on the Bridge Wing.

I was diagnosed with Multiple Sclerosis and my eyes started to deteriorate. In 1992 when I was still in the Navy and five years before I left, I came off the Coventry in 1981, just before the Falklands War. And I went to Chatham for 1 year and from there I went directly to Collingwood to be trained as a leading hand, which is a equivalent to a Corporal's Course in the Royal Marines.

I should have been a St Dunstaner as soon as I left

the Navy but sadly not. *Apparently I just slipped through the net.* A St D's welfare worker visited my home and explained what St D's was all about and asked me to go down for a week's assessment. I had an enjoyable time but Steve as you know yourself, from previous visits, a lot of the guys are older but that doesn't present a problem, You still have a superb time.

The St D's Surveyor, Mr David Rowe and the welfare lady Sue Pryor searched all around until they found me a suitable bungalow. It had taken them approximately 18 months to find me a suitable one and it's perfect. 'We all have a tremendous amount to be grateful for, so thank you St Dunstans!'

I do travel to a gym three times per week as most of the St Dunstaners do. They all complete a rigorous schedule like you do Steve, depending on their own personal complaints. I support local Charities and I also worked for the British Sports Organization for the Disabled for approximately two and a half years and that was most enjoyable.

CHAPTER 9

American Life Insurance Co (ALICO)

When I moved on from the supermarket chain I did apply for a job with commission only. My feelings at that time were that if it did not work I've always got the Royal Marines to fall back on. Well I had always wanted to join the Marines and it certainly made me extremely fit. A school friend who I see occasionally knows I always talked about joining when I left school and he's now a policeman.

Well this gigantic man came prancing and shouting along the corridor in my parents' house and I instantly knew that this was the job for me but I admit it was like knocking your head against a brick wall at first.

Bob Ostler was a fantastic Sales Manager and he could sell snow to the Eskimos, so I had a good teacher and the way he sold was amazing. I was a little bit anxious, wondering if I would actually be able to be successful in this difficult profession.

The train pulled out of Newcastle Central Station and travelled to the Capital. I had to get to Croydon. Once I had arrived I settled in and just got my head down, desperately thinking of what lay ahead I rose next morning and just walked the fairly short distance to this huge tower and apparently that was the home of American

Life Insurance Company (ALICO). All the recruits received a superb volume of information about the Company and you had to study and memorize the script of the Personal Accident Plan because when you first go into the field you will need every scrap of information you were taught.

It was an American company and as you can imagine it was very vocal so naturally I fitted in quite admirably. Most of all you were instructed to be positive. You were informed to have a positive mental attitude (PMA). I don't know what happened to everyone else on the course but they all said they were going to be successful and I made Sales Manager at the quite young age of 21, so why did I sign up? I've answered that small question! I've got this to state: 'The next time an agent from ALICO comes through the door at least listen to him or her'.

What I was taught I practised and consequently it turned out pretty well. All except the bloody truck. After a week of very difficult and tiring training we all parted company and went our separate ways.

Monday morning came around at a rapid rate of speed. I had the whole weekend to relax but it's never enough especially when you are grafting.

The first morning and I met a whole catalogue of different salesmen. Our Manager was present, Mr Bob Ostler, and he conducted the morning meeting. Little did I know there was to be a Monday night meeting in the vicinity of the area we had been working in. We were all designated an area (patch) where we would be working and you received a selection of Lead Cards to visit previous clients to make sure they had no problems. Bob handed out maps of the designated patch you were working with all the shops and industrial areas were highlighted. We should ask to upgrade them to a more substantial policy or better still ask if they know of any family or friends who may be interested. Always work the referral system. It is essential. If you want to be successful there are five points to remember – to own a car, be positive, professional, be able to adapt to any situation and be enthusiastic. Bob and I started work, going in every place of business – what an abysmal response we received! Of course they had seen it before. We visit the area every six months to a year; to visit previous clients and to gather new business. Bob kept telling me to be positive.

We proceeded into every place of business. Bob would do a Dem (Demonstration) of the policy first and I would follow suite. We had copied the script of the policy into our brain. I was extremely fortunate because I had been blessed with a photographic memory and we would need every inch of it. Bob said when you go in the shops you seem to scream and march in as if you are still on the parade ground. 'Good Day, is the proprietor available?' and if so 'I believe this will interest you also.' The whole presentation of the policy used to follow so I used to make the client fully aware of what they were actually covered for and to what degree the exclusions didn't cover you for.

Bob carried on, 'Steve you were definitely an exception. You seem to put as much energy into your work time as you put into your spare time, (there wasn't much spare time). You were certainly very busy. As the expression goes, you took to selling the PA (Personal Accident) Policy like a duck takes to water.'

The idea was to try and sell three policies a day, which added up to 15 policies per week (which is called a 'String'). It doesn't seem much, three 'Yes' answers per day but it was constantly very hard. You had a weekend to do what you pleased and that was cool. If you did achieve 15 Policies per week you were doing bloody marvellous. At the Monday night meeting we all got together. All the various Sales Teams, which covered a vast area from Northumberland through the North East and down to Cleveland. Prizes would be handed out and you would express your congratulations to the salesman or woman who had gained a string or had generated the most business. When there were any new additions to the plan or any new members you would ask some sales person to give a presentation and also to sharpen up on our training.

Also the basis of the meetings was to explain any new information about the PA. The Company would sent Bob information so that all members of American Life Insurance Company (ALICO) were informed about it.

I hadn't been at the Company long but already I was showing potential for the future and as a result was promoted to Area Sales Manager at the quite young age of 21. In return Bob was promoted to District Manager and I was his most successful Area Sales Manager. I was awarded the area of Northumberland and then I was told to recruit. I had some difficult applicants. You were told it was necessary to own a car, but unfortunately, many members came without a car and that was pathetic. Being a salesman with no car is like a canoe minus a paddle. We used to interview in the Swallow Hotel in Newcastle. Bob told me I had leadership qualities and I proved that. My most successful applicant lived near to me. He was a skilful climber and came to visit me when I was down South at St Dunstans. I lost all my records after the injury but if I can recall correctly I think he was called John.

Hexham was a beautiful place to canvass and we received a superb response. My companion and I targeted all the shops but we had only an average response. Then we turned our hand to the back street garages and the industrial area. My mate was working one side and I was canvassing the other. We both had a fabulous rate of 'Yes' answers, which would add up to be a great week. I used to canvass factories and garages but when I wasn't in Northumberland I was master of the self-employed lads on the building sites.

I admit it wasn't necessarily class business but it was a way of getting my String. Taxi Firms are also a good source, as they don't receive an income when they are injured and just sitting at home. Let's face it you are never in hospital longer than a few days. For the self employed, it is essential, but you don't have to be self-employed to sign up. This particular policy pays on top of any additional cover you own.

A word of warning. Make sure you don't have to be actually admitted into hospital before you can make a Claim. You don't with ALICO.

A Sales Meeting would be held in Scotland approximately twice yearly. At that time the North East 'belonged' to Scotland and a man called Hugh was in charge. All the District Managers had to answer directly to him but he was a great man and everyone liked him.

One particular Christmas I travelled up to Aviemore on my own in the great Cavalier 1.8 Lxi, which I had just recently purchased from a mate's garage. I set off early to miss the traffic queuing at the Tyne Tunnel. It was a considerable time before the new A1 was established. Just driving through the traffic was bad enough without the horrible disgusting sleet and snow. I nearly ran out of juice but I just made it to the hotel at Aviemore. The whole region was present. All of our trips to Scotland were very memorable and as soon as we arrived all the Managers were in the bar receiving maximum refreshment.

The very next morning I went Clay Pigeon shooting with our leader and I think he was certainly impressed with my shooting. That same day, in the afternoon to be exact, a Sales Meeting would take preference over all other business. Hugh began: 'When I set targets, I expect them to be met. Only the North East has managed to meet with its figures. Head office will not be happy!' The snow was beginning to lie hence there was quite a lot of activity going on in the small village. People were attending to take part in skiing and to look at the scenery.

Sales people and Managers would stand at the front of the room and tell everyone present how they achieved their sales. You were encouraged to be enthusiastic about life; consequently that transferred over to your sales. When it was Bob's turn to step forward and collect his award he was singing zippy-do and dancing merrily around the tables.

The hotel was very luxurious and enjoyable and it was a smashing venue for a sales meeting. You had worked constantly all year so you were entitled to a small bit of relaxation and nobody knew the pressure on you to actually meet your targets. It gave you a headache. Another sales meeting completed, everyone parted company and went their own separate ways home.

The sales were not going very well in Edinburgh and as a result an injection of some fresh techniques were needed, hence I went up there for one week. I had gone again without complaint. My District Manager had instructed me to assist and so being me, I couldn't very well refuse. I followed my boss up to Edinburgh. We arrived and I got myself booked in and we went for a meal and then we returned to the hotel. At this point

Bob shouted PMA and then he was gone with a wave of a crop!

Well I was the obvious choice, being top sales person, to canvass the area. The first shop I visited I didn't receive much response but at the second I got an overwhelming amount of 'Yes' answers. I had a tremendous degree of success. I moved on and had some lead cards for a glass company. I introduced myself and did the presentation 'Good day. Is the proprietor available or the Manager? Failing that, is there anybody of authority present today? Fine! I believe this will interest you also. What is it? I'll show you.'

Returning to the hotel, I literally forced my training kit on and went running round the hills near to the great Castle. That week I established quite a phenomenal amount of business. Needless to say I received my String. When you gained your String any additional policies could be kept for the next week's business. Often if you achieved 20 you were awarded prizes and these consisted of vouchers and awards for different stages if you accomplished your String. Soon after I returned to the North East and reported directly to my boss. I continued with my role, just working in Northumberland.

Northumberland was very prosperous because of all the business I had generated.

American Life (ALICO) have supported me whilst recovering from this tragic experience. They have encouraged me throughout and I was actually invited down to Bradford to give a speech to all the various sales teams, which was very beneficial.

It was excellent when you were field training a girl, especially when you walked onto a building site. It wasn't solid business because builders were more prone to claim but in their defence it was the type of graft they did. All the workers were making obscene gestures with their hands and wolf whistling but they were only having a laugh. It's not every day a girl walks over the site. When we approached we received a fantastic response. They all wanted the bird to show them the policy, as you could imagine. Most men adore all women especially if they are fit and gorgeous. If you had the choice I'm sure you would pick the girl. Can you blame them?

CHAPTER 10

The Final Chapter

One Night Jimmy Haley came around to tell me about his career in the Royal Marines Reserve:

I joined the RMR in March 1978 and this was quite a considerable time ago. Well I was the fastest Rct (Recruit) to actually achieve my Green Beret at our Unit. I was extremely fit Steve, as you can appreciate.

In the summer of 1979 we saw service abroad in Holland and that was with A Company from our Unit. We stayed at Dawn Barracks and from there we went to the Island of Texo to take part in some Amphibious Training.

We did this at the Netherlands's Naval Marines Base and we were constantly participating in Beach Landings out of LCVP (Landing Craft Vehicle Personal).

Soon after this I went to my second home. Needless to say I went to Arctic Norway because the Royal Marines are frequently touring Norway. I did go there with 45 Cdo to a place that was next to Narvik.

Then I returned to Norway to take part in the second phase or the Winter Warfare and Survival Course. In the olden days if you wanted to be Arctic trained you had no choice but to attend with the Regular Corps but now the Royal Marine Reserve run a Course of their own.

I did a Parachute course down at Brize Norton but

sadly I broke my ankle carrying out one of the jumps. Unfortunately I didn't complete the Para course so therefore I didn't receive my Wings. Not long after this I went down to Poole to train as a D3's (Driver 3rd Class) and I completed this in 1982. If you recall this was the time of the Falklands War. The RMR was not used in the Falklands but they were used to take the places of their regular counterparts, to guard installations and bases etc. Well that's if you volunteered.

The year was 1983 and I transferred from A Company and joined up with the Raiding Trp. I did a Coxswain's course in 1984 and that was the first part of becoming an LC 3 (Landing Craft 3rd Class), basically that is what a Marine would be. In 1985 I did the second part of my LC3s and that meant I was a fully qualified Landing Craft Trained Rank. This enabled me to Drive Geminis, Rigid Raiders, to be a Crewman on a LCVP (Landing Craft Vehicle Personnel) and also a LCU (Landing Craft Utility).

I have achieved a considerable amount with the Royal Marine Reserve. When I was at Harchstad with 539 Assault Squadron I actually piloted a Hovercraft, and that is exceptional. You have 2 big pedals and you press the pedals and this releases the air out of the sides and as a result it digs into the water and that is what turns it. The rudder is just there primarily to guide it. How you do it, is to inflate and deflate the sides of the Hovercraft.

There was always one Cpl and 6 Marines, and if you wanted to receive promotion you were informed to leave Raiding Troop.

The Raiding Trp had five Trps, consisting of Tyne, Scotland, Bristol, Liverpool and London. The strength was approximately 35 men plus a Sgt Major who was in charge of all five Raiding Trps. Also I went to Norway six times with A Company and the Raiding Trp and I went to Belgium as a driver and that took place in 1983 with the RMR.

Training in Hong Kong was very limited but I still managed to go twice.

I was attached to 3 Raiding Squadron in the Far East in the Year of 1987, stationed at HMS Tamar which was on Hong Kong Island. We had been searching all the ships for illegal immigrants and of course drug runners before it was handed back again to the Chinese.

When we were in Hong Kong we were at this large Naval Base and we were using Ribs (Ridged Inflatable Boats). Another name is Sea Riders, which had an engine on the back, (a 1–40 Engine), a rigid hull boat with an inflatable tube round it. This was a cross between a Gemini and a Rigid Raider. We also used Fast Pursuit Crafts and these were called Ribs as well; Ribs were made out of Glass Fibre.

Finally Bill Wright talks about Operation Safe Haven, the humanitarian operation at the end of the Gulf War:

I was with 45 Cdo at that time. We received an order to deploy to the Gulf. At first we all thought we were going into an Arctic environment, but sadly not! Shades was the order of the day, It was Redders (red hot). Well there was quite an amount of snow on the high ground; hence it did come in cold later at night. I was a Mountain Leader 2 and a Cpl at that time.

Most of the Iraqi Army had flown by the time the Royal Marines arrived, and aggressive Patrolling was *needed. The so-called Secret Police were hanging about but they soon dispersed when they were confronted by Royal. The Royal Marines were tasked to make a Safe Haven and clear all the Area of Secret Police. Just our presence had the Secret Police hurrying away for any means of transport. We had to secure the entire village before we could then go into the Mountains and bring all the Heads of the villages down, because they wouldn't come out of their dens unless they were absolutely certain there were no Secret Police lurking around. Once we had moved out all the Iraqi Police, This would enable the Royal Marines to bring down all the families and then they would have to go through the agonizing task of re-building their lives. Even the CO was on the ground, confronting the Secret Police. They rapidly moved away.*

We headed south and that was where the Americans were guarding the airfield. We still had to be re-supplied with certain materials. 45 Cdo continuing to protect all the Kurds because the Iraqis were persecuting them and starving them into liquidation. Sadly the Iraqs thought the Kurds had no place in their civilization.

Once we had established our little HQ then we went basically to assist the Kurds in rebuilding their houses. So all the ex tradesmen got accustomed to their past Civi (Civilian) professions one more time. The Iraqis totally wrecked the village. It was so unusual because we would plan to meet all the men folk in the village centre and ironically only females turned up. We didn't realize that the men brought the money in and the women did all the graft. It took us a considerable amount of time to actually get our heads around that.

We had two separate objectives – to protect the township and then run a vehicle checkpoint. Well, we still had Iraqs trying to infiltrate the Kurds high in the mountains of Iraq. So we literally had to stop and search every car. Anyone we caught we would detain and then hand them over to be tactfully de-briefed. The Iraqi Secret Police were armed but they would try and conceal their weapons, they were right devious individuals. The people with money would try and actually sneak in and bribe their own to turn on their comrades.

It was absolutely tragic because you could see them a mile away, all the Kurds in their horse and traps and these tycoons in a bloody Rolls Royce or some type of Toyota. We used to work with the Kurdish Freedom Fighters and we would have one with each section; they were a bundle of knowledge and they would pick out any Secret Police.

The locals drove like maniacs, and the roads! Well there weren't any roads; they were just dirt tracks with no road markings. Put it this way, no vehicle would ever pass an MOT in that country. Unfortunately that fateful day we were 75 miles adrift through no fault of our own.

That's how I was seriously injured whilst attempting to get the convoy on the correct route and played no apparent role in the Operation ... and the rest is History!